Weaving Our Way Beyond Patriarchy

A Womancraft Publishing Compendium

*Compiled, edited and with an introduction
by Lucy H. Pearce*

WOMANCRAFT PUBLISHING

Copyright © 2024

Each author remains the copyright holder of her own piece of writing/artwork. Womancraft Publishing are the copyright holder of the title, cover and anthology as a body of work. For permission to republish any piece of writing or art in this Compendium, please approach the contributor (details at the back of the book). For permission to reproduce the Introduction please contact lucy@womancraftpublishing.com

All rights reserved. No part of this publication may be reproduced, distributed, or transmitted in any form or by any means, including photocopying, recording, or other electronic or mechanical methods, without the prior written permission of the publisher, except in the case of brief quotations embodied in critical reviews and certain other non-commercial uses permitted by copyright law.

Published by Womancraft Publishing, 2024
womancraftpublishing.com

ISBN 978-1-916672-02-4

Weaving Our Way Beyond Patriarchy: A Womancraft Compendium is also available in ebook format: ISBN 978-1-916672-03-1

Cover design, interior design and typesetting: lucentword.com

Womancraft Publishing is committed to sharing powerful new women's voices, through a collaborative publishing process. We are proud to midwife this work, however the story, the experiences and the words are the authors' alone. The views expressed by each contributor are solely their own and do not necessarily reflect the views of Womancraft Publishing.

A percentage of Womancraft Publishing profits are invested back into the environment reforesting the tropics (via TreeSisters) and forward into the community. 10% of the profits from this book are shared between: TreeSisters, Women's Aid and The Malala Fund.

Contents

Introduction	1
The Weavers Gather	11
Unravelling History	29
Breaking Silence	57
Healing	79
New Visions	111
Prayers, Practices and Rituals	147
Contributors	163

Introduction
Lucy H. Pearce

Womancraft Publishing was founded on the revolutionary vision that women and words can change the world. We act as midwife to transformational women's words that have the power to challenge, inspire, heal and speak to the silenced aspects of ourselves. We share powerful new voices with new visionary ideas, empowering our readers to actively co-create cultures that value and support the female and feminine. This to us is deeply exciting and powerful work.

When I re-read this founding statement I wrote ten years ago, I feel a mix of emotions. Pride at the vision, humbled and exhausted by the daily work it takes to try to live into it and a sense of gentle pity for the naïve starry-eyed younger woman who wrote it. And yet, I decided to err towards this vision, and to mark the ten-year anniversary of Womancraft Publishing we are living into this founding statement even more deeply, publishing this anthology of over eighty women's voices and visions of how we might weave our way beyond patriarchy.

It is a project even more urgent today than it was ten years ago.

The title of this anthology is *Weaving Our Way Beyond Patriarchy* – what exactly do I mean by patriarchy? I will refer you to my book, *Burning Woman*, where I say:

We live in a culture that is only just, in very recent history, opening up to the possibility of women as equals. Ours is a culture that has been built, ruled and inherited from father to son – in heaven as on Earth. This is the patriarchy, literally meaning, 'the rule of the father', a social system 'in which males hold primary power, predominate in roles of political leadership, moral authority, social privilege and control of property; in the domain of the family, fathers or father-figures hold authority over women and children.[*]

---

[*] en.wikipedia.org/wiki/Patriarchy

Ours is a culture in which the masculine is the norm. Both genders in our culture have learned to suppress signs of the feminine in order to survive and be accepted, which has led to a hyper-masculinised culture of men... and women. And we have been taught to 'perform' the feminine in order to gain approval, sexual attraction and power. As women in Western culture, we have been taught to value more masculine traits and denigrate, disregard or trivialise more typically feminine ways of being.

We at Womancraft believe in the power of women and words: many women, many perspectives. The lie of patriarchy is that there is only one (white, male, heteronormative...) truth, that it is agreed upon, and may be spoken of only by experts. We believe there is power – and more truth – in a community of collective voices, each bringing their own lens, their unique perspective, each weaving through their own strand of lived experience, research and soul knowing. This is what we offer you here...not answers, but perspectives that you might try on, ways to see differently, if only for the couple of minutes that it takes to read each piece. Different ways of seeing lead to different ways of knowing, lead to different actions.

This project has been a rekindling of a spark of hope for me. From childhood through to my mid-thirties I was a utopian dreamer. I truly believed that we could co-create a bright new world, that we could transform and heal.

And then the last few years happened.

Breakdown on a personal level at the same time as historic breakdown on a global level. I remember one day I was curled up on the path outside my home in one of the worst autistic meltdowns of my life. Every step I tried to walk to get inside, my nervous system would collapse in another wave. I felt something inside me break. The hope that I had been holding onto for years that things would get better in our personal circumstances had gone. It seemed so dreadfully naïve.

On a collective scale, the complete disruption of normality that has happened in local waves, and then the total disruption that was the pandemic, have led to a subsequent loss of hope for liberals and progressives, left-leaners, alternatives and New Agers. There is a sense of things being totally out of our control: Brexit, Trump, Johnson, Putin, the rise of the far right, the pandemic, waves of cancellations and the culture wars, school shootings and police killings in the US, the total lack of action on the climate crisis, the brutal wars in Ukraine and Palestine...all these have led many of us to retreat entirely from trying to make a difference, feeling powerless in the face of so much violence and conflict.

During the compilation of this Compendium, we were moving towards the decisive end of a dispiriting battle of the elderly patriarchs in the 2024 US election drama. It felt like an unasked for rerun of the previous two election cycles. Neither candidate was a good choice – one whose mental faculties appeared to be failing him, the other just convicted of not one but thirty-four felonies, and both of whom were more than a decade over retirement age. The dinosaurs were holding on, in petty wars of words over who would beat who on a golf course, meanwhile real wars, funded by America, rumbled on. Said one anonymous US citizen in the wake of the attempted assassination of Donald Trump: "We're fucked – I'm feeling less and less like we have a choice and more like the choices are being made for us."[*]

This is a sentiment that people from all political persuasions would echo right now the world over. Disillusionment brings waves of conspiracy theories in what disinformation researcher Amanda Rogers calls "a self-sustaining spiral of shit".[†] There are plenty of people who move from a sense of powerlessness to power by stepping into violent action, in fact there is a whole movement of them, referred to as accelerationists, who see this as the perfect opportunity to contribute to our culture's demise by creating chaos and violence, but are wanting to impose an even more disturbing culture in its place.

Feeling powerless is psychologically dangerous for humans. It is a dynamic that patriarchy has exploited again and again throughout history. Keeping people apart through shame and fear is a tool of oppression and control which ensures the continuity of the status quo. Silencing dissident and othered voices is probably the most used page in the playbook of patriarchy. The other is violence – foster it, encourage it, breed discontent, fan the flames of frustration, start wars, let the people take violence into their own hands and stand back and watch whilst it burns. This is where we are now: male violence and violent rhetoric dominating our daily lives and looming into the future.

Despite much progress for women in the twentieth century, women's voices are still being left out of important global conversations. In the week I put out

---

[*] theguardian.com/us-news/article/2024/jul/13/trump-rally-shooting-political-violence

[†] theguardian.com/us-news/article/2024/jul/14/cool-heads-needed-as-political-fringe-dwellers-spread-disinformation-after-trump-shooting

the call for submissions for this book, it was revealed that on the COP29 committee (in charge of spearheading the next round of international climate talks) there was not a single woman. Out of 28 people.[*] To face the biggest crisis our species ever has. Not one. And whilst we're at it, there has still never been a female leader of the majority of the world's superpowers – USA, China, Russia or Japan (in the modern era)[†]. Out of 195 countries there have never been more than 18 countries led by women at the same time[‡]. The same goes for religion – fewer than half the Christian religious organisations in the US have had a female leader. Once. In their history.[§] And this is only counting the religions that allow women in leadership roles. Women's voices – ideas, insights, needs – are still missing on every level, in almost every field of human endeavour.

The status quo is breaking down. As my friend Tracy says, "these are the death throes of the patriarchy, love, this is what it looks like."[¶]

Alone we might feel powerless, hopeless…but together…

We have seen what happens when women stand together and speak out – think the Suffragettes, the women of Greenham Common protesting the storage of nuclear weapons in the UK in the 1980s, the waves of feminism, #MeToo, VDay, Pussy March, Black Lives Matter, the women in Mexico, India and Canada who have stood together and said enough to the disappearance, murder and rape of women and girls in their communities, the women in Ireland demanding justice over the Catholic Church's use of the Magdalene Laundries and the cervical smear scandal. Something powerful is unleashed when women raise their voices together, awareness comes to what has seemed intractable. When enough women join together and keep calling out injustice, keep standing against violence, the status quo begins to shift…

And how quickly things can shift. As I was writing this introduction we were witness to this – an assassination attempt on one US presidential candidate, and

---

[*] theguardian.com/environment/2024/jan/15/cop29-climate-summit-committee-appointed-with-28-men-and-no-women-azerbaijan

[†] axios.com/2020/03/10/international-womens-day-leaders-political

[‡] statista.com/statistics/1058345/countries-with-women-highest-position-executive-power-since-1960

[§] pewresearch.org/short-reads/2016/03/02/women-relatively-rare-in-top-positions-of-religious-leadership/

[¶] Lucy H. Pearce, *Burning Woman*

a Covid infection for the other, followed by finally listening to his party's calls to resign, gave us the US's first woman of colour as a major party candidate. She was swift in rounding up massive funding and the largest Zoom call in history where over 160,000 women gathered virtually to pledge their support. This is the true nature of change, it is not necessarily steady or even visible – it can seem like nothing is happening and then suddenly, to quote the title of an Oscar-winning film: everything, everywhere, all at once.

My vision for this compendium was to put women's brains, hearts, lived experience, ideas, dreams and insights together to create a document of hope and power that will carry us through the next few years – psychologically, energetically and spiritually. To tap into the collective power of the Womancraft Publishing community to create a volume of practical tools and ideas on how we might travel these tumultuous times with hope in our hearts. How can we cultivate the seeds of the new, growing them up strong under our stewardship and build strong communities that can hold us all?

This book is the answer to that call.

There are many metaphors woven through this book – the image of the womb growing new life, the image of the seed, cultivation and growth, of rising up. But our guiding image is that of weaving. Weaving was traditionally a women's activity, one that created the literal material of daily life – the sheets that were slept on, the clothes that were worn, the bandages that closed wounds. It is one that women seem to return to again and again, one that seems archetypal to us. As those of you who follow my work know, the lost archetypes of the feminine are a driving force for me.

If we follow this archetype of woman as weaver back in ourstory, we discover that:

All mother goddesses spin and weave… Everything that is comes out of them: They weave the world tapestry out of genesis and demise, threads appearing and disappearing rhythmically.

Helen Diner, *Mothers and Amazons*

Just as the mother goddess was moved from her primal role as creatrix of the universe, so were all things considered female or feminine. The idea of women's work was denigrated over centuries, to refer only to the domestic sphere, to the trivial and the mundane. Woman as weaver was demoted from sacred world-maker to demeaned housewife. The public sphere was dominated by men and the masculine. Whilst that tide has been turning, its residue remains, like an oil slick over the pebbles of our lives, giving a strange unnatural sheen that somehow women's actions, women's thoughts, women's voices, women's feelings are just less…important, significant and relevant. We imbibe this poison until it becomes our self-belief.

The reclaiming of the power of the metaphor and literal act of weaving has been an ongoing project for women artists, writers and thinkers throughout the twentieth and into the twenty-first centuries.

> *Across the world from culture to culture, century to century, weaving was – is – both a practical and a spiritual, as well as a creative activity.*
>
> **Jennifer Higgie, *The Other Side: a journey into women, art and the spirit world***

Earlier in the chapter, Higgie makes the point that the term 'textile' and 'text' both come from the same Latin root, *textere* meaning to weave.

This is our work here together – women creating, weaving a text together.

To weave, first you need thread and the time and space to follow the thread of your own thoughts, something denied so many women who, having had their nurturing, or paid work devalued, find themselves having to do it all. Unvalued.

The term spinster was one that for centuries was used against women, to refer to a woman who had failed in her (God-given, culturally endorsed sole role) to marry and have children. They were the ones who spun yarn and lace. I love radical feminist Mary Daly's reclamation of this term.

> **Spinster** *n: a woman whose occupation is to Spin, to participate in the whirling movement of creation; one who has chosen her Self; one who is Self-identified; a whirling dervish, Spiraling in New Time/Space.*
>
> **Mary Daly**

This is what we are here to do together.

We start with the weavers gathering: our contributors speak to what we are here to do – the weaving – summoning our hope and courage for the task ahead. Then we move on to unravelling the threads of patriarchal history and where we've been. From there, we explore the power that is unleashed in the unravelling as we raise our voices and break silence. We then explore how we might heal and transform old patterns and instigate change: practically, energetically, linguistically, psychologically, systemically, politically…so that we might weave in new ways. We then showcase new visions and patterns for how birth, education, motherhood, marriage, health, society and leadership might look post-patriarchy. We reflect on how we can each divest ourselves from patriarchy, evolving beyond violence, fear, shame and the -isms as tools of control and oppression. We end with prayers, blessings, rituals and ceremonies to empower us spiritually, energetically and magically as we weave our way forward in the days ahead.

Some of the pieces in this book are written by Womancraft authors, both established and upcoming, others are from female authors published elsewhere, and many from women who have never had their work published before. They range in age from twelve to over seventy. We hear from authors, activists, artists, community builders, doctors, doulas, priestesses, poets, permaculturalists, professors, teachers, witches, yoga teachers, mothers, grandmothers and more about what it might look like beyond patriarchy and how we might get there – from the big picture dynamics to the domestic details. I heartily encourage you to take time to read their biographies at the back of the book, to follow their work, reach out to them in sisterhood, to weave real life connections and collaborations. It has been wonderful to see that this Compendium has been the prompt that many women needed to revamp or start their own websites and social media profiles, looking forward to making connections. Putting your writing out there, creating on online portal can be nerve-wracking – but my own career has been testament to the fact that this is a powerful way of making beautiful connections and real life happenings.

When compiling this Compendium I wanted to include the widest possible range of voices and perspectives that were submitted to me. This means that the voices and styles (and spellings) differ, and often the perspectives actively clash. For some, the end of patriarchy means a period of only women in power, for others it means an all-out women's strike in the face of violence, for many others there will be a spiritual shift or an energetic realignment of masculine and feminine. There is an urgency to these words, a desire to uplift, to challenge, to celebrate and empower women in every area of their lives. I hope you will agree with many of the contributors, and find yourself nodding in recognition, crying with a sense of being seen and even laughing out loud. But I also hope that you find yourself angry, shocked by what they say or how they say it, stunned even. You may well find yourself putting the book down and taking a deep breath, and then grabbing your phone to share your thoughts with a friend. This is how the submissions impacted me. I hope you get the whole gamut of emotions from anger to joy, peace to sadness, hope to hopelessness. I hope these pieces make you – first and foremost – feel. Feel deeply. For this is the antidote to patriarchy – feeling it all. Every single bit. Not bypassing feeling, as we have been programmed to do.

But feeling is not enough. My dearest wish is that this feeling crystalises into empowered action to make positive changes, to stand up against injustice. This book is taking action by financially supporting organisations already doing the work of weaving beyond patriarchy, or dealing with the mess that patriarchy creates. What will you do?

What is clear is that, unlike in many revolutions, there is no hunger for bloodshed. Not one woman calls for this. This is unlike any revolution under patriarchy. But what will challenge us for sure is how we learn to come to consensus, to make space for differences of opinions and needs – in recent years issues like trans rights and abortion have fractured women's organisations. Can we find a way forward together? Can we, as a collective, as a culture, find ways to transition to a post-patriarchal world with minimal suffering, without economic, societal and environmental collapse? Without more othering and oppression?

Many of us have been brought up on stories of praying to God the Father to save us, waiting for our prince to come or submitting to the greater wisdom of our husband or priest to guide us. We need to move from this way of being and into our own agency. But we must also recognise that we cannot do it all, nor do it alone, in the martyr-mother myth so many of us have learned to embody.

This is uncomfortable work, challenging work. It will require us to speak up, stand up, act out, be unpopular. This is not the time for being nice, biting our tongues or not rocking the boat. And yet these are also not times for making enemies or picking fights. Can we find other ways of engaging and challenging, visioning and contributing to transformation? What might these look like? This book shares many examples.

But first must come a turning point for each of us, a decisive moment when we say, if only to ourselves: I have had enough of things the way they are. I will no longer stand by, I will no longer uphold the status quo, I will no longer stay silent. Things need to change, and I hold within me the power to make changes – even if at first it is only in my own life.

*

I recently read an article about how information is the key to the post-capitalist economy and I realise that this is what Womancraft Publishing manifests: spreading new paradigm information which will inform new ways of living. It was only when reading this article that I realised how revolutionary our business is, in giving a platform to potential new culture makers and shapers, and in choosing to operate a different business model to any other publisher I know of. We share powerful new voices with readers, so that tens of thousands of women every year engage directly with new visionary ideas, taking that information in and birthing it out into the world through their lives, their work, the way they build their own personal cultures and contribute to our society as a whole. This to me is deeply exciting and powerful. Values are not meant to be dry words, or feelings, but juicy actions, lived out. Books are not meant to be mere paper, but the means of transporting ideas from place to place. Business should not just be a way of making as much money as possible, but a way to consciously change the world, one transaction at a time: by what we choose to make and sell, and what we choose to do with the money this generates.

This all feels doable when we are thinking about our own individual lives – but what about the issues that now face us: impacting patriarchal capitalism and climate change require collective action? The fate of the Earth, of Western culture, is a force far bigger than any of us. Its threads are complex and knotted. To think we can change the world is naïve…and egotistical. It is certainly simplistic.

There is a strong bent in Western thought towards apocalypse and the fall of humans – from Judaeo-Christiantity to cults to environmentalism to far right leaders. It often feels as though many in these groups are willing disaster to happen in order to prove themselves right and to clear the decks for the fulfilment of their own prophecy. The fall of our culture is often depicted as inevitable, divinely intended, with this world as simply a finite passing place. Those who focus on trying to make things better for the people who are here now, and for future generations, are simply rearranging deckchairs on the Titanic.

I ask us all to reflect: what do we mean when we say "change the world"? What do you mean? This big, vague promise was used to inspire and mobilise people in the twentieth century when it was the rallying cry from hippies and despots. The question for us now in the twenty-first century, as we witness the death throes of patriarchy, is not "how can we change the world?" as a massive action, by force of will, at some unappointed time in the future…this is the endless lie of governments, reformers and rebels. No, the question is how can we live well now? How can we embody our beliefs and values more completely each day? How can we create community here, with the people to hand? Rather than decry or ignore those many different folks we share our geographical communities with, wishing for the ideal, like-minded folk we would cherry pick for the utopian community we dream of. How can we create now? What will we create? Who with? This is not to say that we don't consider our greater environmental and political impact, that we don't think of the future – we should and we must – it is something patriarchal culture has been remiss at. But most of all we must think – and feel – broader, wider, deeper, wiser, always paying attention to the larger pattern, both warp and weft. We must keep on weaving: whilst there is breath in our bodies, and the sun in the sky, there is hope. Let us weave it through our lives and communities…creating beautiful new patterns in the cloth to keep us warm on cold nights and to lie on the sun together on summer afternoons. Creativity, community and hope will take us far, whatever the fates bring. These should be what we return to. These are what we must practice: creativity, community, hope. The time for fear and inaction is past. Let us commit to no longer freezing in the face of uncertainty, playing dead, or waiting for someone else to save us. Instead let us commit to taking creative action with hope together. There are no right answers. Perfect will never appear. Let's talk and listen, gather and make, and rest. This is perhaps the most rebellious act against patriarchy. Rest.

Then feel.
Then vision.
Then take action.
Alone and together.
In sisterhood,

Lucy H. Pearce, Shanagarry, Ireland. August 2024

THE WEAVERS GATHER

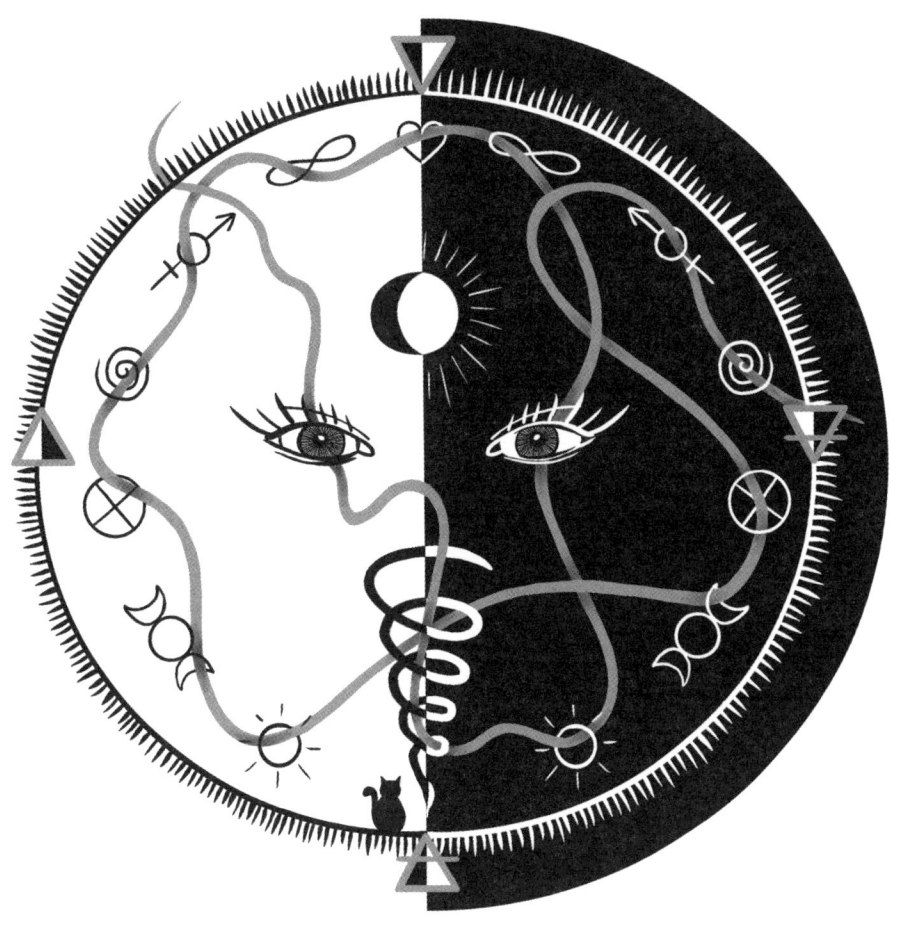

The Witch
Liset Dettingmeijer

Forecast
Coco Oya Cienna-Rey

We are being awakened out of hibernation mode. The years between 2024–2027 are going to be huge activation years. The entire cosmic, planetary, biological and galactic bodies are shifting. A multidimensional shift is taking place. What within you is calling to be heard? What is calling to be loved back into being? What part of yourself have you neglected? What dreams have you not allowed to pour through into the now? What desires have you let slip away out of your reach and conscious knowing?

To fight the system never transforms anything. We have to remember who we are and that we can eat the dark and turn it into endless fuel for our life force. Know that as you burn bright: you are evaporating and disintegrating the darkness that brings about so much disconnection. We have to ask ourselves: How do we want to experience being here on Earth as this era of humanity closes out and we venture into new territory? What new perspective do we wish to embody so we can move in a more harmonious direction? We get to be the living example of the world we wish to see so that others can make those choices too. As we share information with one another, we become beacons that show others alternative ways of being.

Extract from *Digging for Mothers Bones: a guide to unearthing true feminine nature,* Coco Oya Cienna-Rey, Womancraft Publishing (2025)

What if?
Mary Lunnen

Right now, 'weaving our way beyond patriarchy' feels an impossible dream
And yet, 'weaving' and 'beyond' are two words with so much potential
Two words with feminine grace, and masculine determination
What if?
What if, together, we could do this?

'Beyond patriarchy', beyond fear
Beyond domination, control
Beyond raised voices, and sometimes fists
What if?
What if together we can step beyond?

'Beyond patriarchy', beyond division
Beyond man and woman
Beyond husband and wife
What if?
What if together we can create a new way?

'Weaving our way', soft yet strong
Weaving a new fabric for society
Weaving a life of colour and pattern
'Weaving our way', as equals
Weaving love and care for all beings
Weaving happiness and joy

'Weaving our way', to an end to war
Weaving peace in our hearts
Weaving peace between people

What if?
What if now is the time?
What if together we can change the world?
What if we can weave our way beyond patriarchy?
Shall we try? Right now?
Yes.

Hope Sings in Our Soul

Carol Watts

Hope is that thing inside us that insists,
despite all the evidence to the contrary,
that something better awaits us if we have the courage
to reach for it and to work for it and to fight for it.

Barack Obama

Just as Raven is known as the trickster of the bird family, I think of hope as the trickster word in the English lexicon.

The tricky thing about the word hope, I feel, is how easily it can be confused with optimism. This is hope with a small 'h' – a wishful thinking kind of hope that slips out of our mouths in idle conversation. This is usually a hope for something completely and utterly out of our control, and it may be difficult to reconcile when our problems are not always solvable. Hope does not begin in a place of favourable circumstances, and hope does not guarantee a positive outcome.

But, there is another, more mighty hope. The hope with a capital 'H'. This is the Hope that, as Obama referred to as: "that thing inside us that insists…that something better awaits if we have the courage…to reach for it, work for it and fight for it." I would name this the hope of possibility. This goes way beyond optimism and wishful thinking. It is where we can step up and be positive agents of change.

Recently, when meeting with friends to share tea and conversation, I became aware of how often we uttered the word 'hope' as we mused over world events. I think we all used the phrase 'I hope' in the context of wanting things to be different. We talked of the headlines on the evening news that told of horrific conditions for refugees of war. We discussed, at length, the doom and gloom news of melting ice and starving polar bears, of climate change and warming oceans – of extinction. We felt fear, despair and anxiety for the world our children and our grandchildren would inherit because of the breakdown of civilization as we know it.

We seem to be a society, especially in the West, that is reluctant to look back and learn from the wisdom of the Indigenous peoples whose ancestors' wise ways stewarded the land for many thousands of years. Precious resources included all life: air, water, rocks, minerals, plants, animals and humans. We hope our politicians will act more urgently to find a peaceful solution to the ravage of wars and tackle climate change. Yet, many of us are so overwhelmed we sit back and wait for them to take action as we have been conditioned to do.

Lily Tomlin once said: "I always wondered why somebody doesn't do something about that. Then I realized I was somebody."

As I reflected on the earlier conversation with my friends, I recognized that as we witness the daily bombardment of fearful news from politicians and climate scientists, our hope cannot be placed in those who continue to fail us while busy with their agendas. Hope is ignited and powered within us, inscribed in our hearts. Can we remember we are here to serve one another, to honour and respect all life, and to alleviate suffering by using the tremendous gifts we have been given?

Our ability to harbour hope is the most profound, innermost aspect of our existence. It gives us a sense of purpose and the courage and energy to take action. It can serve as the guiding light to see the possibilities for change in the darkest times, providing a sense of direction and the motivation to keep moving forward. All it takes is a spark of determination to ignite the flame that allows us to envision a better future for all beings.

Every challenge presents an opportunity for transformation.

We can become immobilized by the big picture. Yet our incremental small acts toward a hopeful future make a huge difference.

So, is it possible to have hope? Yes, absolutely. Hope lies in our capacity to change, innovate and work together for a common cause. It's about seeing the possibilities of even our most minor actions and trusting in our potential to rise to the challenge.

Emily Dickinson once wrote, "Hope is the thing with feathers that perches in the soul – and sings the tunes without the words – and never stops at all." So, let's keep that song of hope alive, for indeed, that is love in action as we strive for our vision of a better future for all life on this magnificent planet.

Women Who Weave and Gather
Kelle BanDea

My mother's people, the Mincéirí (Irish Travellers), tell an old story about weaving women. This camp of travelling, foraging women wander the land, gathering bark and plants, wool and flax into baskets made from willow branches. This they then spin and weave into cords of blessing for newborn children, until their woven cords encircle the world.

This is more than a cute folktale. This is a tale about women who weave blessings and visions for the generations to come. Who gather the threads of the old stories, the stories of our ancestors, of the land, and of a time when we knew in our bones that all of these things are connected.

Moving beyond the wounds of patriarchy will not mean going back to a mythical time of the past. That is why the women in the tale weave blessings for the youth, so that they can pick up the threads of the old stories and carry them forward, retelling and reweaving them in new ways for a new world. Restoring – restorying – what has been lost and cutting away what is no longer needed, or has been actively harmful.

This image, of women working together, gathering up parts of the past in order to plant the seeds of something new, is one which has stayed with me ever since I first heard the tale. For in the figures of the women themselves, I see a model for what a new world could look like. One which has us working, loving and living as reciprocal communities, without hierarchies, with a deep and abiding respect for all; for our ancestors and descendants, for our elders, our youth and our middle-aged, for our various genders, ethnicities and neurotypes, for the land and the other-than-humans with whom we share it. One where we weave together all our stories: of love and loss and heartbreak and happiness, and dare to dream of new endings and new beginnings.

The old heroic sagas of the past do not work anymore, if indeed they ever did. Creation myths that give humans – white men, mostly – dominion over the earth have caused great harm. In the folklore of my mother's people the land is a friend, a home, and the ground of our being. It cannot be owned or carved up or staked a claim upon, and when we try to take more from it than is our fair share, the consequences are dire. These are the things that the women who weave know and remember. The warnings they pass on to the children; to keep your footprints light. Walk softly upon the earth, for you tread upon your Mother.

I dream of a world in which this knowing is so bone deep that to imagine otherwise seems ludicrous. Where the heroic sagas have given way to community songs that everyone knows the words to. Where each generation picks up the threads of blessing and carries them forward, weaving a tapestry that belongs to us all.

Warp and Weft
Mary Lunnen

There are two very separate and distinct parts to a woven piece of fabric.

Warp thread: this is the thread that is strung over the loom vertically and holds the tension while you weave.

Weft thread: this is the thread that you weave between the warp threads, creating your patterns and structure in the weave.

Reflecting on this, for me, offers a path to experience the masculine and feminine differently.

Holding the tension while you weave – this feels like a masculine aspect, an active doing, holding.

And then the weft feels more feminine, with flow, creating your patterns and structure in the weave.

The essential aspect for me is that neither warp nor weft is more important than, or superior to, the other. Both are an integral part of the weaving: both play their part in the pattern, the colours, the structure. Neither would be anything but a collection of threads without the other.

I can see now how I can apply that to the balance of masculine and feminine within myself. Sometimes I resist the call to hold the tension – and, oh my goodness, that word – tension. I feel as I write how I have labelled tension as bad, unwanted, even painful. What if it is an essential part of the reweaving of a new world, in the same way as it is necessary for the cloth? Can I hold that for myself? Can I allow others to hold it for me too?

Then when it comes to being the weft: creating patterns and structure – can I allow myself to flow, to play, and at the same time to be consistent, dedicated in what I am creating, able to complete the process?

If we – as individuals, as communities, as humanity – if we are able to embrace this equality of importance, equality of opposites – literally up and down, and side to side – will we then, together, step beyond patriarchy, into a world of new opportunities and joy?

For many years I have worked with the image of 'weaving shadow and light'. Acknowledging the gifts we find in those parts of ourselves we may label 'shadow'. As with 'masculine' and 'feminine', there is no right or wrong, no good or bad – simply the differences that make us all wonderfully diverse human beings.

Maybe we can replace patriarchy with a new pattern, a tapestry? Within each of us, and within the world?

Weaving
Kate Ward

Weaving a path beyond patriarchy takes on a more practical meaning for me as a fiber artist that specializes in abstract woven tapestries. The process of creating through joy is so counter-intuitive to what we've been conditioned to do in a capitalistic and patriarchal society. So counter-intuitive in fact, that I believe it's a powerful form of resistance. My dream is to see more people tap into their well of sacred creative energy, and forge ahead with small businesses that can sustain them with not just infinite amounts of joy, but financial stability outside of oppressive capitalistic institutions.

Dreaming This Tapestry
Jennifer Miller

Even if we don't know how to weave,
even if we have no loom yet,
we are each holding a thread
and dreaming this tapestry into life.

We send forth our poems and prayers,
our paintings and our visions
for this emerging world,
revealing itself one layer at a time.

We sing up from our roots,
and the sound carries
over mountains and seas
to the ears of all who are listening,
waiting, watching, knowing,
ready to offer another strand.

We invite every color, every story,
every piece of ancient wisdom distilled
down from a time we can't remember
any other way except in our bones.

Lifting the Veil of Suffering
Eve Smith

Beyond the veil of the Patriarchy there is magic. A beautiful place that hums with vitality, strength, connection, and joy. It is a place where the flow of life is clearly seen and understood in a way that brings us deep wisdom. From this place of wisdom, we are brought into Harmony.

Balance.

When the world is seen with our full senses aligned to the way that it moves and flows – all is possible.

Like with any endeavor, to access this wonder, the veil of fear and attachment must be lifted repeatedly and over time until its hold is loose enough that the veil may be removed entirely. With the removal of fear and attachment, we are released from their child – suffering – as well.

From that point forward, our entire world shifts.

Born Necessary
Sarah Durrant

When the fabric of your deep belonging
Feels lost, unravelled
Too cheap a trade has been made
The warp and weft, the weave of us
For frayed threads, I and other
They offer little warmth
Even less to pass on.
Put them on anyway
The work of shouldering bodies
Into the dead valley
On your way up the mountain
Is a cold business
If you knew of the welcome
The villaging
The hearth in your bones
Would you loan one moment longer
Your bountiful, mendable heart
To this tyranny?
If we each remembered the gifts we carry
That each
Into this life
Is born necessary
We'd walk more slowly
Every moment would be a
Meeting in the jewelled marketplace
Where no-one is selling, no-one buying
Everyone bowing
And bowing and bowing
To the unending light in each other's eyes

Longing

Rev. Jo Royle

I long for a world
Where we admit our mistakes…
Mistakes of the past, mistakes of the present
Not hiding them, lest we be blamed
Taking responsibility
Thus no longer clinging, perpetuating the same damaging cycles
day…after…day…after day

I long for a world
I long
I know you long too
And in that longing
And knowing you are longing
I feel be…longing

Let us long together, belong together
Because it is in our longing and belonging
That we will bring into being
Our longed for vision of the world
Let us long for not just a different world
But a better world
A world in which we all belong

Extract from *Longing*, Rev. Jo Royle.

Stepping Into Ourselves
Rachel Glueck

The Patriarchy is crumbling. We can see it in the state of the world. We can feel it in the rage of women, in the heartbreak of men, in the confusion of our children. Who today doesn't feel as if humankind is teetering on the brink of an abyss? Unlike in past decades when things looked pretty grim, but we still believed there was a way forward, most of us today feel utterly hopeless when faced with the world's ills. But that is only because the familiar fallback no longer serves.

Hope lies in a new vision we are only just beginning to build. Men and women will be a part of this creation, but it must be women – it can only be women – who lead the way. Our task is no longer to push or pull reluctant men into a new way of living and being. Our task is to step into it ourselves, whether or not they choose to follow. We begin where women have always begun: in our hearts and in our homes.

I'd like to offer some tips for hearing our own voice and creating a vision for the future. These small, but powerful actions have worked for me in this process, and I hope they are helpful to others.

- Connect with nature.

- Give ourselves time and space to hear our own voice. That could mean going for walks alone, dancing, practising an art or sport, or any number of things. Mostly it means spending time alone without distractions, doing something we enjoy.

- Gather and share with women we value more often, more deeply.

- Deeply consider our personal values – not the values of others we've adopted. How are we meeting them? Where are we falling short? What small actions can we take to integrate them into our lives?

- Become deeply critical of the systems and culture we're immersed in and have accepted. Pause before accepting another's premise. Question everything. Most of these evils are so entrenched we've lost sight of them. How can we push back?

- Get rid of the TV or carefully choose the books and programs we expose ourselves and our children to.

- Teach our kids to listen to their own wisdom, to enjoy time alone, in nature, allowing them to play with random bits they find rather than flooding them with plastic toys.
- Listen to our intuition – cultivate it, follow it. Teach our children to do the same.
- Don't put up with the B.S. Draw your boundaries. Stand up, say no.
- Embodiment practices and exercise work wonders. The first, to know and ground ourselves in ourselves; the second, to let out the rage.
- Get angry. Show your anger.
- Journal. This is where it all comes out. I often find myself stuck and floating, knowing the resolution is there somewhere but is evading me. Until I start writing – not with the goal to resolve it, but just to let it all out. Resolution comes naturally.
- Discuss the hard things with a sense of curiosity and openness, not shame.
- Trust ourselves.

Discovering our power and stepping into it is the most difficult part of our transformation. But that power is like the pull of the moon on the tides: once we know it, everything follows.

21st Century If*

Victoria Nangle

If your house is riddled with rot,
If your child tantrums for years,
If your family are cruel with words –
over three turkeys in a row,
If your circle betray your trust –

---

* Referencing Rudyard Kipling's celebrated poem, "If" (1895), which begins "If you can keep your head when all about you Are losing theirs and blaming it on you, If you can trust yourself when all men doubt you, But make allowance for their doubting too…" and ends "Yours is the Earth and everything that's in it, And – which is more – you'll be a Man, my son!"

And ignores your hurt,
If your friends don't listen as they shriek and twist,
If your world is tumbling down all around you do you wash your hands of the lot of them?
Join in the howls and terror?
Or run away to another land and start again –
As if you played no part in the construction of its cursed predecessor?
Or will you stay?
Will you go where kindness is lacking and demonstrate kindness?
Show those who have lost sight of compassion what it looks like?
Bring corners of frivolity and sunshine to the depths?
Recharge, breathe deeply, and step outside each day.
Hole up too when you need to.
Treat that rot.
Sit with that child.
Try another turkey with your bloodline…
Or even just pick one action of Hope.
Stay and live your life the best way that you can,
And keep that minority percentage we have been left with in play.
Protect your home, your love, your land,
From falling even further.
Is this the worst you can imagine?
Or the worst that you can endure?
Stay.
Stay by my side – if you can.
And together let us demonstrate kindness to each other,
So the 'others' see it's real,
And one day mimic it –
As children do.

A More Beautiful World Awaits
Linda Sewallius Katz

A more beautiful world awaits

   And she's not far, not flung into the distant future or waiting in some ancient and untouchable past, she is under my nose and my feet, pulsating through the lacy leaves of wild carrot that tickle my sockless soles and stir my senses awake, it is she who calls to me through the blue sapphire spring morning with the voice of the redtail hawk cutting clear through the din of rush hour traffic and people racing to begin their workday and pool pumps whirring and leaf blowers blowing away last season's death into thick black plastic bags before it is ever given the opportunity to break down and give birth to new life

A more beautiful world awaits

   I feel her heartbeat in my chest as the midday summer sun bakes my bare skin, the light so bright I have to squint until my eyes are nearly closed, my eyelashes becoming curtains shielding me from the intensity of the beauty on full display as the chorus of cicadas rolls through the live oaks and cottonwoods, wave upon wave, the swan song of their brief life on earth washes over me as the heat rises up from the parched ground and sings to the sky for a storm to quench its thirst

A more beautiful world awaits

   Lounging like a kitty cat in the honey-soaked evening light that bathes the trees in gold while I sink into the slow and steady breathing of my big gray dog lying beside me, gently lifting her nose to catch what moves on the breeze that I cannot sense with my animal body but only imagine in my mind's eye, as my own belly softly rises and falls, I ponder what a strange and miraculous gift this moment of life is as the autumn leaves drift gently down, released from their seasons of receiving and producing to be given as an offering of what is yet to come

A more beautiful world awaits

   Hidden in starkness of the winter night where the waning crescent moon is nestled into a blanket of stars, tucked in for the evening and shedding little light on the obscure landscape below, while the cold wind whistles through the inky black and barren branches unhindered, carrying news of snows from the north, and I wrap my arms around me more tightly and bow my head more lowly as I listen for the haunting hoo-hoo of a great horned owl that seems to come from all directions at once, a testament to this bleak and lonely night that I fear may never end

Yes, even in this desolate dark, a more beautiful world awaits

Not to be born, nor for the breaking of day, nor for the sprouting of the first buds of spring because this world does not wait like a promise but as a presence who lingers and prays that we may open our eyes and finally see

The beauty that is already here.

Crab
Poppy Connor-Slater

Imagine it
a hermit crab transfixed by its shell
the countless failings of the shell are gruesome,
growing larger, the iron weight of it drags the crab
to the bottom where she dreams only of new shells
forgetting that the soft flesh beneath
is formed of shining gold and dotted about
with moonstones like the eyes of heaven
and that the shell has for so long
held her safe incased in pearl, and how
within the degrees of its spiral
are written the laws of the cosmos

That was how we lived then
You ask me what changed and I tell you that
one day the weight of the pain grew so heavy
that we cast it all off like so many capes
They fluttered there in the wind one still moment
and vanished entirely

Looking outside we saw
it had never been the shell that was wrong

but the poison water all around
The great mountain stands always by the river
its meltwater, crystal pure as siren song
will wash away the poison, given half a chance
And we, cape-less as we were
were more than half

This Woman is Rising
Looby Macnamara

This woman is rising out of the ashes
Into the brightest of flames
This woman is rising into a roar that fills her crown
This woman is rising to say NO to violence against women
And to say YES to our strength
This woman is rising to tell her story and to rewrite herstory
This woman is rising to connect with herself
And to be her full self
This woman is rising to be with sisters of every colour,
From every country, to be a global community
This woman is rising because it is essential to the world
For every one of us to rise
This woman is rising because she was hurting
And to take away the pain
This woman is rising to walk her own path
This woman is rising because she has the opportunity
And to welcome the possibilities
This woman is rising for the One Billion[*]
This woman is rising to feel her joy, to feed her passion
And to dance for freedom.

[*] One Billion Rising, organised by V, formerly Eve Ensler.

Dance Free *Elen Jones*

Beyond patriarchy,
Is a time,
Is a place,
Is a motion.
Beyond patriarchy, is a dance floor.
Fred Astaire, gliding, tapping, smooth-as-silk.
Dodging, the old spectres,
And making shapes, in air.
M.C.Hammer, moving, his trousers full of pomp. Silly, but fun.
The patriarchs, have dry mouths,
They barely move, at all.
They hover, at the edge of time.
Sober.
I, and my posse, drunk on love, move.
Here, comes Divine.
Her body strong, powerful, tender, brave.
She rolls her eyes.
The patriarchs shiver, melt, become hot.
They'll make a law, next week, against eye rolls.
You know it, girlfriend.
But, until then, I, am here, on the eternal dance-floor.
Where boy, meets girl,
Where man and man kiss, in movement.
Where woman, is sassy, bold, and free.
Or delicate, and supple.
A ballerina, is far beyond, always.
Who can subjugate the free world, in a tutu?
All dance, is mine.
All song, except the driest hymns, the slowest dirges.
And even they, have notes.
Notes dance, on the written page, my love,
When not pinned down.
And the patriarchs are a tired bunch, with so much work to do.
The patriarchs, my dear, always leave the party early.

                                        Extract from *Dance Free,* Elen Jones.

UNRAVELLING HISTORY

Turning the Tables

Hazel Evans

We're Still Here
Molly Remer

First we relinquish our names,
trading identity
as we step into someone else's
fatherline,
leaving behind the nameless chain
of women who spun our cells into being.

Next we surrender our soft bodies
and let layers of our dreams
slip away
into suckling mouths
and sticky fingers,
our tenderest flesh scarred
and leaking,
while we carry new dreams
curled and sleeping,
bundled against us,
even tied to our shoulders,
as we feel our way
through the long corridors of change.

They forget, you see,
that we come from those who
created art and agriculture,
those who gathered what they could
and who wove the threads together,
created life instead of weapons.

We come from soil and story,
the discovery of bread and fire.
We come from all that could be preserved

to feed our children another day.
We come from sunrise and from gardens,
from libraries and song.
We come from lines of sweet jellies
shining jewel-like in the sun.
We come from a patchwork of tenderness,
strength quilted together with determination
to survive.
We come from long slow years of
experimentation,
hands curled around the faces of the sick,
tinctures dropped across thin lips,
as we persist in brewing together
what we can make of hope.
We have come through famine and fatigue,
laid our hands
on wet earth
and shaped it into vessels
that can walk through fire.

We have crossed continents and
nourished countless generations
with our bodies, breath, and prayers.
And, we remember.
We remember to create and not destroy,
to connect and not coerce.
We remember how to dance and sing
and weave and write.
We remember how to howl and hug
and love.
We remember how to cast colors across
the page
and how to make meaning
from sticks and threads
We plant our feet on a living earth.

We lift our arms to an open sky.
We watch for moonrise
and listen to the night.
We weave our threads together
into stories that honor the nameless
and share the secrets
and that persist in making the world
more beautiful and safe
from each of our own small spots
in the web,
hands extended,
eyes alight,
bodies worn but still standing here
together.

We come yet bearing culture
in our hands,
the art and stories
and longings and loves of people,
of what matters most.
We know seed songs
and moon dreams.
We know heart dances
and hip openers,
we know how to roar new lives into being,
to spin cells into stories
and grain into life.
We will carry what we can,
we will remember what we know,
and we will not stop singing,
we will not stop writing,
we will not stop dancing.
We will not stop our healing hands
from feeling,
from piecing broken shards

of meaning back together.
We're still here,
part of all that survives
to keep telling the story,
to keep carrying the art,
to keep making what magic we can.

The Fifty Maidens and Apollo
Kelly Barrett

Karen, the program chair of my department, who was normally quite animated, simply looked stunned and sat silent for a full twenty seconds before she responded. And then she asked, "Have you ever considered an alternate ending?" I burst out laughing. It had never occurred to me how dismal the event I just shared might sound.

We had been having a lively conversation in which she was helping me identify a research topic that I would be passionate enough about to sustain me through the long year of research and writing ahead, my final year in the MA program in Consciousness and Transformative studies. Something in our conversation sparked a memory from my first year in the program when I was researching the symbol 'peacock' as part of a course called Symbolic Process.

One day, huge stacks of random books had been piled on a table for our investigation. Perusing indexes for "peacock", I landed in the book *Mothers and Daughter of Invention: notes for a revised history of technology* written by Autumn Stanley. On page 96, what leapt off the page was this short descriptor of a purported event:

> "at least one group of fifty maidens drowned themselves rather than be ruled by Apollo"

My breath caught as I felt an inexplicable recognition, a powerful surge of resonance. It was truly a lightning bolt moment.

According to author Elise Boulding, cited by Stanley, there were other stories of mass drownings and this, he suggested, hinted of a time of dramatic takeovers by men. In my bones, although there was no specific evidence of this event, I was convinced it was utterly true.

I was born in the 60s into a family with conservative and traditional values that did not align with my understanding of who I was or who I was becoming, even as a little girl. I secretly and not so secretly raged against the misogyny I witnessed at home and in my culture. Thus, it is not surprising that a story of this nature, relayed in one mere fragment of a sentence, invigorated me. I loved the rebellious spirit. It conveyed a sense of strength, a righteous, hell yeah, Thelma and Louise style conviction. For some reason though, I had not thought of it in tragic terms. And no, I had not considered an alternate ending, but perhaps that was not an unfit idea.

I mean, why did I think suicide was bad ass? Obviously, I loved the decision to not serve Apollo and applauded it, but suicide? Anyway, this entire anecdote became the animating spark initiating my research project *The Great Magic: Rewilding the Feminine,* with six other researchers in tow. Through revivifying the instinctual feminine, practicing in our daily lives, we began embodying an emerging living story of what was possible in the world of Apollo. In what ways could we live according to our desired values, not serve Apollo, and not commit suicide? Ultimately, I offered an alternate ending. Instead of drowning, the priestesses (aka fifty maidens) arrived at a differently shaped relationship with Apollo, one of partnering rather than domination.

My interest in the 'drowning event' did not end with the culmination of my research paper in 2018. Indeed, you might say it continued to haunt me. When I was living in Manhattan in 2019, I spent many hours in the New York Public Library research room, possessed by the need to prove this event had occurred, that it was not just some anecdotal reference as many people gleefully tried to suggest. On some level, I felt an obligation to the memory of these priestesses, who I believed had existed, to rewild their story back into contemporary memory. Even now, in 2024, without fulfilling my obligation, I still continue to carry this story.

Recently, I woke up with a new realization. Maybe I had not been right in seeking an alternate ending in Herstory, for wasn't that what the patriarchy was fond of doing? Rewriting history and eliminating Herstory? What if what was recorded as suicide in a Patriarchal culture was also a liberation and a new birthing of possibility in Herstory? After jumping in the waters, what if they did not drown? What if they vigorously swam? And yes, they had chosen to commit patriarchal suicide by deciding to no longer participate, but they were also simultaneously being born into a new world.

Now I am contemplating it as a *continuing* story, not a revised ending:

"at least one group of fifty maidens drowned themselves rather than be ruled by Apollo" Or at least this is what Apollo and his cronies witnessed and reported. Yet, this is not where the story ended. The maidens, all strong swimmers, defiantly left one shore forever, and swam in the waters of an unknown ocean to an unexplored shore, ultimately arriving in virgin territory, building something vital and new.

Athena's Truth
Kimberly Moore

They called me cruel and heartless. And I let them.

They assumed I was capable of radical betrayal. And I let them.

Millennia have passed, and I am remembered for petty revenge and jealousy. And I allow it.

But even Gods grow weary and, as smiting has fallen out of modern favor, I am reduced to watching irrational men wage their irrelevant wars. No honor, no strategy, no victory. Perhaps I am thankful that they have forgotten this Goddess of Warfare. But I digress.

"It is time, Mother, to share our story."

Her soft whisper fills me with gladness and sorrow in one crystallized moment of grief. Our story. My Beloved Medusa and me.

Are you surprised to hear me call her Beloved? Centuries of propaganda has been successful.

I close my eyes and in a flash, I am there again, on the terrace of my great Temple. As I surveyed my city, the sound of tormented weeping reached me from inside the sanctuary. One of my novice Priestesses, Medusa, had collapsed in front of the altar, bruised and broken, with blood staining her gown.

We held my Daughter as we bathed her, whispered gentle reassurances, and had her sip wine with herbs to calm her and ensure no pregnancy would come of the rape. Even as I stroked her brow, I was filled with rage. The clouds began to roil over the city and lightning spidered across the sky.

Once Medusa was asleep, I requested the presence of the Gorgon sisters, Stheno and Euryale, to watch over our charge. Finally, I indulged in my fury and burst from my Temple, intent on vengeance.

My uncle, I spat. The great earth-shaker raping a young Priestess barely out of childhood. He was a defiler of my Daughter and the sacred boundaries of my Temple. My spear itched to relieve him of his pitiful manhood.

I searched and searched, and the coward eluded me. I had just turned my consciousness back to my Temple when I heard an otherworldly screech, and a shock of golden light vibrated through the aether. I knew immediately what that light meant. I reached to my waist and the thunderbolt was not there.

We had not realized the depths of her sorrow. The damage to her mind. Her fierce determination to not be a stain upon the Temple. Her primal fear that she would never be safe again. She thought to just burn up, like a phoenix, and so she grabbed the thunderbolt.

Magick is not predictable. It is wild, chaotic, primordial, and that magick sought out the clearest thought in Medusa's mind: that she wanted to be fearsome, and she wanted to be safe – and, watching the Gorgon sisters, she knew few could go up against them.

The shapeshifting magick of the thunderbolt carried out the impetus of Medusa's mind in front of us all. Her long spiral curls began to pull up into her head; weaving and darting serpents emerged. Her feet and hands expanded and clawed. Her shoulders broadened and leathery wings appeared at her back. While the Gorgon mask did not appear across her beautiful face, I knew the power of those paralyzing eyes.

Absolute silence engulfed us. We were all reminiscent of the stone consequence of those eyes. Medusa's Gorgon body carried none of the wounds her human body had suffered. She sat in the silence, absent-mindedly stroking her serpents as though she'd always had a hundred snakes emerging from her skull.

The Gorgon sisters embraced her as if they had birthed her themselves. And for a time, Medusa seemed to shed her fears and her vigilance.

But that is when cowardly men strike.

In one fell swoop of an axe, Poseidon's agent of her assassination, Perseus, sliced Medusa's head from her shoulders. As I arrived at the Gorgon's sanctuary in Sarpedon, he was standing over Medusa's body while Stheno, Euryale howled and stalked him. Then the fool snatched up her head and began wildly wielding it at me. ME.

Me, a Goddess.

Me, the agent of his destruction.

His face was red and sputtering, his impending doom causing him to jerk and screech, a possessed puppet. Her face was drained of blood, a silent alabaster backdrop to the crimson spray across her cheek. Her eyes were tightly closed and remained so as I took our Medusa from the pathetic little man. The gold light vibrated the air again, as it had that original night. In that golden moment, Medusa's eyes flew open and looked directly into the eyes of her murderer.

He was petrified.

I took Medusa to my aegis to keep her with me, to allow her the glory of being fully Gorgon from the sanctuary of my breast, to remind all that none is closer to me than Medusa.

They have vilified her for centuries, and we let them. They have called her monster and aggressor, and we let them. They claimed I set Perseus on his murderous mission, and we allowed it to stand.

But even Gods and Gorgons grow weary.

And now you know the real story. A new era of reclamation must begin. The golden light of transformation carries Aletheia through the aether, to the hearts and minds of our daughters on Earth to remind them how powerful they truly are.

Justice
Margaret S. Malloch

Where is Justice?
I thought I caught a glimpse of her
A glow in the moonlight, a spark in the darkness
A light along the way
But I must be mistaken
She died a long time ago…
Stoned in the temple
Burnt at the stake

Banished from the village
Cancelled by the culture…
Gone, but not forgotten.
But in my dark night of the soul
I felt a cool breath, heard a gentle sigh
The soft touch of hands on my shoulders
Comforting, reassuring
Giving me the strength to use my voice
To speak my truth
and another sister caught the whisper of Justice
…as she echoed through my words…
And the rumours of her aliveness
Could not be contained
And knowing that one woman had been in the presence of Justice,
…had felt her touch,
Gave others hope
And a sprinkling of courage
And connection to their own deep strength
And to each other
And where we brave souls gather
To speak out and speak up
She will be there too
Here is Justice
We are Justice

Beyond the Garden
Molly Remer

We have come from beyond
the Garden,
stories both old and new
in our hands.
Our breasts are bared,

our hips are heavy,
and we are willing to show
our incisors.
Centuries of silencing
and suppression
have been unable to stick
to our skins,
our lapis beads
rest easy
across our throats,
and red crescent moons
shine upon our brows.
No longer willing
to settle for giving birth
to demons or destroyers,
we bleed all over the pages
of history,
eat all the apples we please,
carve stone into shapes
that tell our hearts
to remember,
and sing
of the forgotten things,
untamed, unbound.
Our most reliable sacred text
is the one we write each day,
shard by shard,
step by step,
bone by bone,
breath by breath,
side by side.

Patriarchal Narcissism
Georg Cook

The patriarchy has, for centuries, thrived on using its tools of fear and silence to great effect. Keeping people engaged in their differences from one another, calling out anger where it is least welcome. Division has been made welcome for too long. This toxic blend of corruption and media led "truth" has allowed Narcissism to grow in the shadows, feasting on lies so readily handed out. The ones shouting loudest are often the only ones heard, unquestioned in their narrative. A deafening crescendo of noise to drown out the margins.

Margins which seek expression, inclusion, creativity and a coming together to build something more than what has been. One of empowerment not entitlement. The tide is turning though and won't be held back. A call to arms has been sounded by Mother Nature and women everywhere are weaving their way back to her. To stand united together as a collective voice of tolerance and inclusiveness. Where ego has been left at the door and open hearts sing together to raise the vibration and birth into being a softer, gentler soul led future.

By women.

The Wounding
Nicole Cohen

Yesterday I watched a father humiliate his daughter. In public. On purpose. He used shame as a power tool – his weapon of choice for making her fall into line and bend to his will. He thought he was doing it in her own best interest. He saw it as a learning experience. I saw something else.

I saw the trauma land. I saw her freeze as her body absorbed the shock of what had just hit her. I saw her hunch in on herself as she tried to make herself a little smaller, a little less of a target. I saw her soul shrivel as she learnt how to take up less space in the world, how to make herself less visible.

She'll survive of course. And she'll carry that scar forever. That same blunt trauma tool of shame and humiliation will be used against her again and again until it leaves a series of ever deepening dents in her heart that will start to fester and rust, to tarnish her sense of self and poison her from the inside-out.

One more perfect soul wounded by the people who are meant to protect her. Those who are meant to nurture and nourish her, to help her grow into all that she already is. Instead they chop away pieces of her until she feels less than nothing and acts accordingly, chopping off more pieces of herself all by herself, their disdain ringing through her axe of self-loathing.

Another blossoming young woman cut down to size. Taught to fit herself into other people's expectations. Smoothing away her rough edges until what is left no longer feels like her. Until the best parts of her are gone, lost forever, and so the cycle continues…

Until we find another way to love. Whispering words of encouragement back into our own souls until we remember the power of kindness. Until we remember who we really are. Until we are ready to love from a place of wholeness.

Witches
Katia Wallace

They burned us at the stake
They buried us alive
They drowned us in the sea
Or in rivers
Just deep enough to take the last breath out of us
Tied to a rock
To make us stay down there
Silenced and bloated
Screamed out and charred
Muffled and rotten

But they forgot that the fish that they ate
Ate me
And the dust that they breathed was the ashes of me
And the food that they grew was fertilised by me.

I am even to be found in the flowers that decorate their homes.
Millions of sisters like me
Resilient and beautiful
Gently passing on our legacy.

We are not dead
For the witches are alive through you and around you
Nothing is lost, nothing is created
All is transformed

Watch me burn
And be reborn
Like the phoenix
Purified

Distilled
Nutrified
The very best essence of me.

Dismantling the Internal Patriarch: A Psycho-Spiritual Approach

Philippa Aspey

'Self-care is how you take your power back'.[*]

The word Patriarchy comes from the Greek; literally meaning 'the rule of the father'.[†]

We know that women have experienced oppression and subjugation in a devastating number of ways for centuries. We are aware of feminist movements,

---

[*] Lalah Delia
[†] Wikipedia

understandable reactions to this level of control. We've learnt about many courageous women who've fought back and stood up to the tyranny. We hold deep gratitude and respect for the women who have shouted themselves hoarse for the cause and paved the way for a future where women have the same rights as men.

We have journeyed far and broken many barriers, but are we where we want to be? And what has been the cost? Still, in 2024, there are many who have yet to experience liberation and exercise their equal rights. There is a deep, deep weariness experienced by those who continue to engage in bringing about this necessary change. And there are, within the feminist movements and fields of sexuality/gender, many cracks and fissures which require our attention.

Activism and campaigning have their place and are as important as ever, but at this crucial point in time there is a need to dive deeper; to understand what underpins this damaging and pernicious system that we are living in, and have all unconsciously internalised, regardless of our gender.

One of the most important things that I have learnt as a psychotherapist is that if we want to see long-term change for the better, we need to begin with ourselves. Not only is it important to *understand* what underpins oppressive and controlling behaviours in others (unprocessed trauma resulting in a deep sense of inadequacy/worthlessness), but to understand what drives our own process in reaction to these behaviours. The imbalance in the external world reflects the imbalance within each and every one of us. Until we examine and align ourselves with our own authentic core values, we are travelling through fog; and this generates fear. As Marie Curie said, "Nothing in life is to be feared, it is only to be understood."‡

Although fear of failure is incredibly common in Western cultures, we have also been conditioned to fear personal *success*. I don't mean success in the patriarchal sense (status, money, material goods) but engaging in a life where we feel fulfilled; a life where we are doing what we love and connecting authentically to others, a life with *our unique Purpose.*

This fear is strongly attached to a belief that we don't deserve to live a life that we want, that we're *unworthy*. On a conscious level you may instantly disagree with this, but dig much deeper and you may stumble across this hurdle.

"Our deepest fear is not that we are inadequate.

---

‡ *The Mental Health Handbook,* Trevor Powell

Our deepest fear is that we are powerful beyond measure.
It is our light, not our darkness
That most frightens us."*

To relinquish the power of the patriarchy therefore, we deserve and owe it to ourselves to examine what we have internalised and let go of what no longer serves us.

It is essential that we make time to rest, recuperate and reset. That we find and/or create safe spaces to be heard, witnessed and with the appropriate support, gently and lovingly 'dismantle' our own conditioning in order to focus on empowering our authentic self.

To examine and question long-held beliefs. To relinquish the striving and relentless pursuit of goals/perfectionism/status/achievement. To release our obsession for being busy and filling every second with 'doing'. To lessen the pressure for 'success', and loosen our grip on the 'shoulds', 'musts' and 'oughts'. To place as much value on intuition, emotional intelligence, imagination, creativity and lateral thinking as we do on reason, rationality, logic and linear thinking. To let go of and transmute our grief, shame and rage and in time, invite others to do so too. Our rage is entirely valid, as are all our emotions, but to get stuck in blame disempowers us further.

To tell our stories in safe places of non-judgement, empathy and compassion. To listen to our own intuition. To acknowledge and honour our vulnerability. To learn active listening and be kind. To prioritise creativity, in any form, for the enriching process that it is rather than fret about the end result. To sit with uncertainty and to trust the unknown. To sit in silence and nature. To transcend polarities. To cultivate compassion, acceptance and a trust in something 'other'. To bring ourselves, then others if they choose, back into balance and *know* that co-operation and community is the future.†

---

* *Return to Love,* Marianne Williamson

† Recommended workbooks that may assist with the healing process are: *The Artist's Way* Julia Cameron; *Mind Over Mood,* Greenburger and Padesky; *The Self-Esteem Workbook,* Glenn R. Schiraldi; *The Mental Health Handbook,* Trevor Powell

Unravelling the Threads of Patriarchy
Lyn Thurman

We live in interesting times, experiencing the death throes of the patriarchy which violently shake the foundations of Western civilisation. Simultaneously, the contractions of something yet to be born squeeze horror into the hearts of men and cultures that only know the toxic masculine way of existing. They fear what comes next because it's still unknown. So, they hold on tighter, control harder, narrow their focus, and battle forward. Collateral damage, no consequence to them, hurts us all.

Empires and civilisations grow then they fall. It's the nature of the world, of everything really, this unstoppable motion of rise and descent. Nothing stays the same, nothing lasts forever. As we duck from shrapnel and falling bricks as best we can, we can choose to call back our power to build from the rubble and ruins.

As women, we are intimately familiar with this liminal space. The place of potential and possibility as the old falls away and the new comes into being. It's a realm pregnant with possibility. The cycles of birth, life and death flow through our being and collide in the present moment. The past dissolves and the future waits to be shaped. Who shapes it? That is for us to decide now.

Patriarchy has wielded the power of this in-between space, this cauldron of change, to dictate our destinies rather than empower us to co-create them. Our rightful ownership of this space of potential has been denied – our wisdom disregarded; our voices silenced. We are the weavers of the future, the hands of the Fates. If we just wake up long enough from this man-made nightmare we can remember this. It's in our blood, a direct link from the Great Ancestress who gave us the power to consciously create, consciously live and consciously destroy.

Dismantling patriarchy won't happen through brute force; there'll be no armies lobbing bombs or totting guns. Rather, it will be through heart-led actions of awakening women who have experienced enough, seen enough and felt enough to know that patriarchal living isn't living at all. It's barely existing. This collective rise of women will spark a million quiet fires that move a revolution.

Unravelling patriarchy seems like an almighty task, one perhaps too big to contemplate. But it needn't be. It's the collective effort of awareness in our daily lives that holds the power to effect change. Each of us holds the potential to be a weaver in this movement. Small acts of personal resistance, such as listening to our truth and following where that leads, ripple outwards. Each heart-felt act of kindness leads to another, an honest conversation inspires one more.

Every social norm we question, every boundary we push, we tug at a thread and undo a little of what has been wound tight. It might seem insignificant at first, but each thread becomes a possibility in the yet-to-be-written narrative of future generations. And for us? We claim back our place in the liminal space as descendants of the Great Ancestress and we weave. We weave hard. Our lives might just depend on it.

Wendy

Mary Cardenas

There are few things more ingrained in us as humans than storytelling. To communicate, engage, share, educate – to evolve; telling stories isn't just in our bones; it's in our energy. But what about the stories we inherently absorbed during our earliest days? That is to say, the stories originated in the mouths of men. These are the fairytales we were read at bedtime and the movies we watched in the dark of a theater with our hands stuck in a candy box…all those times the men who wrote those stories told us to aspire to be princesses who needed rescuing – or worse, adventurers who should choose domesticity over a life of wandering.

I recently read J.M. Barrie's *Peter Pan* for the first time, the story of a boy who wouldn't grow up. We all know it as the tall tale packed with adventure and magic and a girl who got to experience it all but, in the end, still chose to grow up. I'd seen so many visual adaptations of Neverland over the four decades of my life, but they mostly centered around the titular character, Captain Hook, or the Lost Boys. There have certainly been reimaginings with Wendy at the core, but during my reading of this classic, I was surprised by one very Wendy-specific section when I read it: it was Wendy who kept Peter from flying out the window, which is, in turn, the moment that incites the rest of the story. Without that moment, Peter goes home to tell the Lost Boys how another one of Wendy's stories ends, and the Darling children stay in the Nursery, but it is Wendy who isn't done telling stories to Peter, Wendy who craves adventure as much as the

Lost Boys and her brothers. It was Wendy who wanted to keep weaving magic with her words.

All mending of the metaphorical patriarchal socks and shadows aside, I had forgotten that it was not only Wendy's stories that drew Peter in but that she made the first move to keep her adventure with Peter alive. But once she got to Neverland, she took in the behavior of the undergrown boys Peter wanted her to mother, and well…is it any wonder she chose the familiar life awaiting her in London? Who wants to mother a brood of ageless men and be saddled as Peter's maid where time stands still? I know that in the end, she chooses to return home and eventually becomes a wife and mother because, of course, she does – the book was written by a man in 1911. I refuse to disregard everything that inspired me because of its outdated and limited ways. But what I can do is decide to find the spark from each old story that is worth keeping and divesting from the whole of the original. I can read/watch/listen/consume a story like Peter Pan and take from it what I need.

Reading this story made me consider something. Imagine taking back each childhood story we loved and examining it through the lens of allowing the princess, the sister, the daydreamer, the curious – to just *go*. What adventure would they find if their families said, "Go" with a smile instead of shouting after them, "Go, and you'll end up miserable and in trouble!" What if we encouraged our adult selves down to the youngest generation of women to adventure with support behind them? How many dragons would they slay, not just on their own, but with the reinforcement of existing family units and the family they've chosen along the way? How often would they do the saving instead of drifting off into a dreamland where they are told to wait to be saved – to keep cautious and vigilant. I know modern storytelling for kids is changing, and for that, I am grateful, but there are still so many outdated norms and 'traditions' steeped in our society like a stained white teacup; even if you can't taste it, you can still see the residual mess the old drink has left behind.

If words are spells and stories weave magic, the intention behind why we tell a story is the crux that gives it meaning. With every new story we tell, we can provide more representation and layers to stories that shift away from patriarchal values. But what about the stories we were told as children that are already deep in our bones and carved into the inflections of our people-pleasing thoughts? Wendy was the storyteller; Peter needed her, and Wendy loved adventure. She experienced all she wanted until she wanted something different. I don't need to walk away from every story I have ever been told, but I can take new meaning from them. I can still be surprised by them, and now I vow to find a way to take the pieces that matter to me – and make them mine. I'd like to keep what's for me and leave behind what isn't, just as Wendy did.

Scattered Seeds
Rosalie Kohler

The dark shadow of Patriarchy
has razed fertile forests to the ground,
burnt fluidity from the landscape,
leaving a brittle, barren desert.
And yet we endure.
Scattered like seeds on the wind,
barely more than grains of sand,
we cling to the last embers of life-force that we carry within us.

For we know that emptiness will be filled.
We cling to survival in the wasteland,
until the rains come.

Each droplet softening the hard, harsh environment,
coaxing tender life into being.
Root-systems gather moisture,
weaving networks of support with fine fungal threads.

And we grow wild and abundant,
to blossom in a million different shapes and forms.
We are the vessel for a new beginning.

Almond
Shirley Graham

I was two years into my PhD research on women, peace and security, before I found out about the abuse. Up until that point, I thought violence against women was something that happened to other women, not me. I was reading feminist literature about war and gender, and it was taking me hours longer than it should, because I was crying so much. These weren't dainty tears prettily rolling down my cheeks, these were big blobby tears, snotty tears, sobby tears. Many rolled up tissues would be strewn on the table beside me, as I read each article. It felt like I had dived into a deep well of grief.

It never occurred to me that while I was digging into the research that I would come closer to uncovering my own story.

A key goal of feminist research is making the invisible, visible. Discrimination, oppression, gender-based violence, gets woven into the culture and discourse as "just how things are". As researchers we are encouraged to ask the questions nobody else is asking. "Where are the women? What are they doing there? What do they think about being there?" We pay attention to the people that most scholars of war and peace have ignored.

I learnt that the biggest security threat for women globally, is not war, it is intimate partner violence.

Security for women stretches way beyond the confines of violent conflicts, wars, and militaries. Yes, they amplify our insecurity, we are disproportionately impacted by them because of how we are de-valued, marginalized, displaced, raped, brutalized, and killed during war. But the most common weapons used against women are the hands and feet, the penis and the mouth, of a "loved one".

I came to understand that because society normalizes the violence used against women in our relationships, families, and homes, that we often blame ourselves for being victims, and this keeps us silent.

Did you know that survivors of domestic violence have enlarged amygdalas? Our brains change shape in response to our environment, due to years of living with chronic fear. The amygdala, a small almond-shaped part of the brain, never gets to rest. When we are in a dangerous or stressful situation it becomes flooded with the hormone cortisol and we go into "fight, flight, freeze" mode. Why does this matter? Because, one in three women are subjected to physical or sexual violence in their lifetimes, and much of that will be at the hands of someone they know and love.

I began to see the shape shifting power of patriarchal systems and institutions, and how they keep us thinking that we are the problem, not the culture.

The insidious nature of gender-based violence goes beyond physical harms to emotional and psychological abuse. For many of us, the war is not out there, it is in here, as the words we hear over and over again become woven into our inner dialogue. We internalize the sexist narratives of our culture and repeat them through self-rejection, put downs, and shaming tactics that keep us small, contracted, and fearful to be seen in our full radiance and power. The "I'm not good enoughs" becomes the commentary running in the background of our minds.

I became curious about how we can root out our internalized misogyny.

By journaling first thing every morning I began paying attention to what my mind was saying over and over again. Pages of hand-written diatribes against myself, anyone who had hurt me, and all the problems in the world, filled up many notebooks. Sometimes, my rage was so visceral I would carve through the paper with my pen, slashing it to shreds. Other days, I would cry on the page, as all the ways I had bought into the "blame the victim" narrative against myself, became visible.

I saw how I had been controlled by my inner patriarch, and I decided to do everything in my power to divest myself of her critical voice.

As I kept writing I uncovered a quieter, gentler voice, one who was often scared but who genuinely cared about my well-being. She encouraged me to read everything I could about healing from trauma, and reconnecting with my body, heart, and mind. She invited me to dance and sing again, to slow down and listen again, to stand still and feel again. She invited me to share my story with trusted friends, and to see that I was not alone.

I learnt that we can change the neural pathways in our brain by thinking new thoughts, and developing kinder habits towards ourselves.

Through self-compassion and mindfulness I began to think more tenderly about myself, to feel my body, and to allow all of my emotions, no matter how painful. Over time, my nervous system began to relax, and I could focus my mind for long enough to complete my studies. I began to see myself as having agency over my story, and I reimagined how it might unfold.

A new picture of my life began to appear before me, one that was not defined by violence or trauma, one where I was the narrator.

Patiently, I reassembled my story like a jigsaw puzzle, one piece at a time. But I felt like there was still a piece missing. Then one day a voice I had never heard before appeared on the page. She was fierce and kind. She asked me if I would follow her to where I needed to go next. Instinctively I trusted her, so I said "Yes!" She smiled and asked me to open my hand. In it she placed the last piece of my jigsaw puzzle, a perfectly-sized almond.

The Wild Woman Way
Julie Armstrong

Dear Sisters,

I am writing to invite you to walk the Wild Woman Way to reclaim our rightful place in the world, and reshape it through the perspective of the feminine to bring about spiritual, political and environmental change.

But first I must ask before we embark on our task: can you recall when Women shaped their community? We did, it is true. Across ancient civilizations women were intellectual and spiritual leaders. Queen Puabi of Ur, Queen Semiramis of Assyria, and Cleopatra, the last Pharoah of Egypt. Once upon a time, during the Neolithic, Women were respected for their skills, curing ills.

They were story tellers, astrologers, shapeshifters, herbalists, Guardians of the Earth, responsible for birth and death. It was before patriarchy when Women were revered not feared for their insights. Women lived by the cycles of the moon and the turning of the wheel, knowing what to plant where, how and when. They owned property, engaged in trade and initiated divorce without remorse. Then came "original sin" in the Garden of Eden and everything shifted. So, it goes, but who knows, Eve yielded to temptation and ate an apple from the "tree of knowledge." Please, note, she became a scapegoat. The men of the church said sex was the work of the devil and "witches", at their peril, were his agents. The female-centred tribal system fell apart.

But, Sisters, do not lose heart. This is a rallying cry! I do not lie, in the twenty first century an exciting phenomenon is underway. Believe me when I say, Women from all walks of life are awakening to set off on a journey beyond patriarchy. We would like you to come along too. If you do, you will need stout boots, spells, rites, rituals, blessings, a woolly hat, a meditation mat and your innate wisdom.

This pilgrimage maybe a challenge but together we will manage to get from here to there without despair. But we must be united, trust in our instincts and venture deep within, towards the *wild*, our primal side, the world of our imagination. To fulfil our task, we must ask Mother Earth to be our guide. She is the midwife of rebirth. She is the one who will show us how to be part of the whole.

She will nourish our soul. As we walk the Wild Woman Way She will gently remind us to pay full attention to creatures who have so much to teach us. So, like them we can be relaxed yet alert, trusting our instincts, living in harmony with spring, summer, autumn, winter. If we do not already know she will show us how to listen to the whispers of the forest, mountains, meadows, hedgerows and our voice inside, we can-not hide from their advice; it will help us make choices for a better life, one without strife. To make our plan work I must advise you that we must not shirk from our vision, one motivated by intuition and feeling, meaning and healing. And we must all agree that every bush, flower and tree have rights same as us. Thus, the world will be a place of compassion and kindness, not rule-bound and mindless. It will be calm. We are the balm. Walking towards a place of peace and love, not one of domination, control and destruction.

Hand in hand, taking care of the land. As we go, through rain and snow, we will re-discover our roots and nurture the shoots of change. We will feel no shame and will not blame. Instead, we aim to sing our songs and put right the wrongs. It is not about going back in time, it is about embracing knowledge from the past to inform the future.

This is our finest hour to reclaim our power and nurture a sense of belonging. We are longing to rebalance the planet, ourselves and each other. We are sister and brother, no one is "other". We wish for all life on Mother Earth to blossom and grow, thrive and flourish. And we, dear sisters, will nourish and care, always aware, that we are walking to save humankind by weaving our way beyond patriarchy. As I hope you agree: *It is time for a new beginning, a new way of thinking, a new way of living. It is time for change.*[*]

---

[*] Julie Armstrong, *The Magic of Wild Things*, Moonflower Press, 2020, p.185

If you wish to join our journey, please, write back with a resounding "YES".

With love and light and hope,

from

A Wild Woman

P.S. As Swedish artist, activist and author of: *The Great Cosmic Mother,* Monica Sjoo, once said: 'If we are to survive, we have to attune yet again to the spirits of nature, and we must learn to "hear" the voices of the ancestors who speak to us from their Other realms.'
(Exhibition, Oxford Contemporary Art Gallery, February, 2024.)

Contract
Hazel Evans

This New World Contract *(aka magic spell)* is to the toxic patriarchy *(from the witch that will never die no matter how many lifetimes we journey together).*

Dear *(Insert name, e.g. anyone who is a tyrant in any place of leadership.)*
   I am writing to inform you that your current contract has been annulled.
   This is the last lifetime your authority has been adhered to, and due to your repeated breaking of the laws of nature, true justice and love, you are thus released from all your duties as of this moment, (insert date).
   Your time, karmic and all other, in and out of the office, is complete. The tower of your empire is scheduled for immediate destruction. *(Usher in the golden wrecking ball of the golden life.)*
   Due to your consistent refusal to love and honour life, you have left me no other option but to love you even more. I shall do this by withdrawing all my energy, attention, and investments from you and your empire. Love grows where my attention flows, and you have not honoured my gifts to you; therefore, access to my magnificent self is now denied.
   This may be very challenging for you at first, which is why you have been prescribed lifetime compulsory attendance at the New World Rehabilitation Centre

of Peace and Love. You will start the curriculum immediately in the beginner's class. *(See mirror of truth accompanying package.)*

Due to this turn of events, I also need to let you know that I will be loving myself, my family, my friends, nature, my soul purpose and passions more than I have ever done before.

I thank you for the profound and difficult lessons you have been teaching me. I fully accept my self-sovereign leadership as of this moment. I am now the master of my own destiny, and your authoritarian ways are obsolete.

I would like to say it was nice knowing you, but to be honest, it has been really difficult, and I am now glad I and the people I love are free. Adieu.

Sincerely and with love,

(Insert your name)

P.S. This letter will explode in five seconds.

BOOM Message delivered. Mission complete.

Incantation of the Valkyries
Rebecca Houston

'Come, sit with us, let down your hair-
we see your pretence falling
naked now in your need/ just how we want you-
come dance with the all the parts of yourself you lock away
don't you want to let them out, to fly through the night
to burn down all these soldiers
who say battle is the only way-
go away now to the corner
with the night light
sink into the bath

sneak down into the kitchen
go ahead and take a bite
eat it up with your long perfect fingers
we will teach you how to rest/ how to grasp gently/ how to take what is yours/
how to leave enough behind-
for now, take this small pink pill
to soothe the brain and body
for you live in this place which demands:
produce, or perish/
the exhaustion Olympics-
think of those Greek women
who quit fucking men/ stopped an entire war
we want to shove off late stage capitalism
get its twisted hands off our divinity-
such a lie this zero-sum game they have us play
we want to feel, to touch, to taste and dance
share gifts with one another, for
nothing on this whole Earth is ours alone-
look out at the mountains
see the heights we can climb
the abundance in the air-
we want to live like this in the daylight
desire all out in the open/ manspreading, like legs/
let us woman spread
like the Great Mother
like a Bitch who knows
exactly what she needs to birth a universe
we are so weary/ of ushering only warriors to paradise-
we want to play/ a different game'.

BREAKING SILENCE

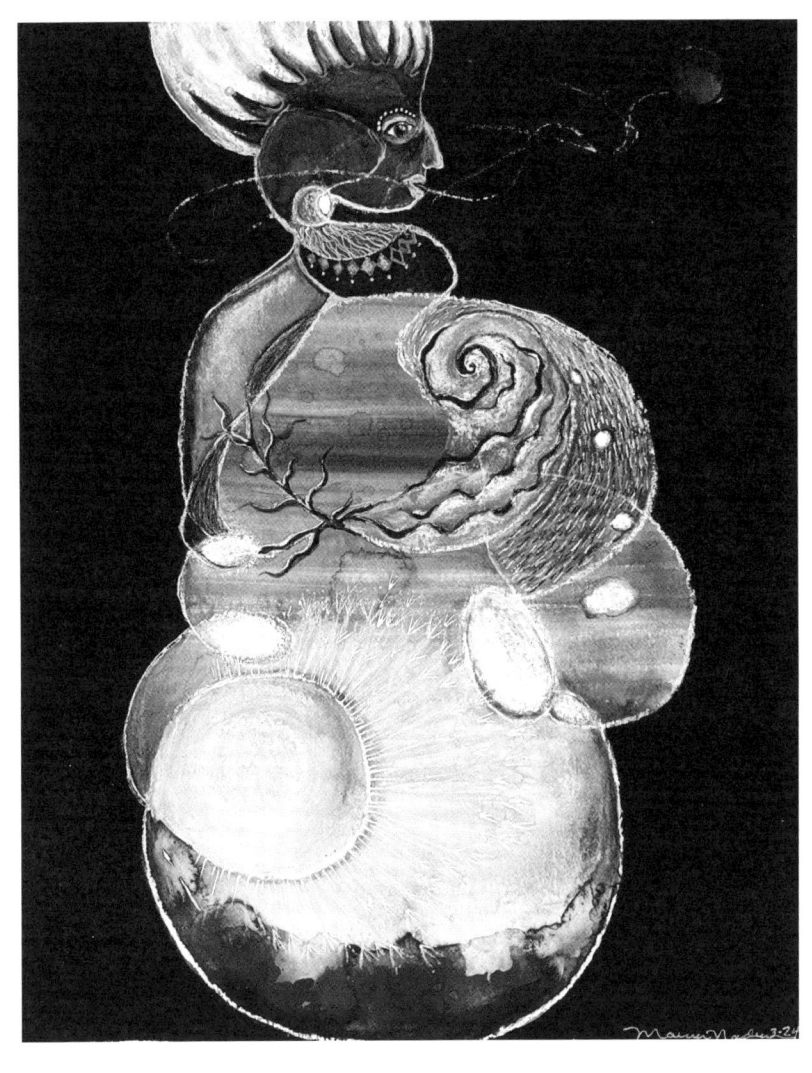

Shine Your Light into Darkness

Maureen Nadeau

A Deep Breath and a Scream
Edel Murphy

"Three women dead. Three locations".

The headlines rolled. Then came the details… A figure in a black hoodie, balaclava, black tracksuit, and black shoes had been caught on CCTV leaving the scene of one of the crimes. The newsreader spoke about a death, by the docks a few weeks earlier, that was now under the same investigation. In a trance she dressed for work, quietly pulled on her parka and headed out the door for the office.

At work the conversations, amongst the women, centred around the deaths. "One happened around the corner from my parent's house", one woman said. Annie, the accountant, told her colleagues how she had walked home earlier last night via the same street one of the girls had died on. Her face was ashen as she spoke. Annie went home sick not long afterwards.

In the afternoon the head of the creative team, James, called a meeting to discuss an advert for a client. He noted how energy was low and he needed the group to 'push on', 'drink some energy drinks', 'play some trance music'. Apparently, 'overtime' wouldn't be a problem! "That cash will come in handy," one guy said. The men in the room laughed, they were pumped up and patted each other on the back. The women were a little less enthusiastic. No one spoke about the attacks. No women stayed after dark.

Sheila, being a senior creative, had to stay late. Home was a 15-minute walk but tonight she called an Uber. While she waited Bobby came in with his bike helmet in one hand and satchel over his chest. "I'm off Sheila", he announced. "You good?" She pinched the place between her eyes, above the bridge of her nose, she looked up and smiled then ushered him out the door with the wave of her hand. Grabbing his bike he smiled back, wheeled it out the door and cycled down the street.

Sitting in the back of her Uber she stared out the window. Groups of lads walked together, no doubt heading to the local pub to watch the big rugby game. Couples linked arms. Dog owners walked their furry friends, standing guard when one had to do its business. At a red traffic light a woman jogged alone across the street.

Once in her front door, she locked up and let out a sigh of relief. The day was over. Two weeks later it happened again but this time only two women died.

The city seemed to have taken a breath and had forgotten to let it out. The evenings grew dark and cold. Chimney smoke filled the air in the suburbs. A greyness had descended that just didn't seem to shift. In the small kitchen of her office the radio newsreader reported the news of two women found dead, both in their twenties. By this stage the murderer was identified as a male, in his late 30s. This was followed by a man's voice, the Chief of Police, encouraging women to not walk alone at night, to go out in a group or with a male relative, just until the culprit was apprehended. That evening six Ubers were called to the office. The men headed home by foot or bike; others just went straight to the pub to celebrate the football match win the night before.

Sheila and her friends spent hours texting each other. Checking in on female relatives. Attending vigils week after week for the dead souls. Nothing changed. More women turned up dead. Finally a rally was called, the women were angry. Their fear had turned into rage. They were prisoners in their own city. The same city where they paid taxes, paid rents, and mortgages, dropped their children to playschool, shopped in local supermarkets and clothes stores. A city that they helped to build and maintain. Thousands of women marched on the streets. Their voices roared with aggression.

The message was clear; "No murderer in jail, then no men on the streets after dark!"

The media gathered and shot photos, live streamed the action, desperately shouted at the leaders of the protest to give a quote. But the women kept screaming.

"No murderer in jail, or we down tools!"

"No murderer in jail, then no men on the streets after dark!"

"No murderer in jail, or we tear this city down".

"We will tear this city down!"

The men in the office stared out the window as Sheila and her colleagues walked past, placards raised high, shaking with rage. Not a word was said among them.

Dedicated to the women of Yorkshire, England.

Opprobrium

Rebecca Houston

I wear this t-shirt, it reads: "well behaved women seldom make history"
   a quote often misattributed to Eleanor Roosevelt but it wasn't her
   it was Laurel Thatcher Ulrich, who told stories of quiet, ordinary things
   I wore it a lot when I was pregnant with my daughter, belly round beneath the words
   we always provoked some kind of reaction/ so many opinions on how to shape a growing girl

A man with a long grey ponytail looks wide-eyed at my chest
He asks: "who is your favourite, misbehaving woman?"
I start to answer he almost/ lets me finish, before telling me the tale of Eleanor-of Aquitaine, I say I do not know her, he smiles from the corner of his mouth: "oh realllllyyyy!?"

Later I look her up thinking about irony and mansplaining and misbehaved women who misbehave
   because men will not stop mansplaining their misbehaviour and calling it misbehaviour in the first place when actually we are just trying to get free

   Anyway, Eleanor of Aquitaine, Queen of France/married at fifteen mother of ten
   ran an empire behind the scenes (like we still do every day)
   then her son became king, of course/ I bet she wanted to stab everybody in the neck
   do you think the old ponytailed men would have noticed?

This one, he goes on to say: 'a man can never sweep a woman off her feet, if he does, he's a chauvinist'/ I think at first he's right, for dust is a thing to be swept and I have been dust eyes underneath rugs/ fingers shoved inside me/ asking for more, more, more/ dissolving, until sneezed violently, out/ out out
   These days I stand on my own/ I have legs, I have a man who does not try to

take me out at the knees-
   but what do all these ordinary men know about Desire?
   of longing, to Plow it all over
   to have someone run their hands through you like dirt

A Plea from the North Wind
Adele Mower

I am not angry
I am seething-furious
a Fury with feathers and fags.
You have left us behind.
Forsaken.
Forgotten.
Found wanting.
Diminished and disregarded.

We are not the daughters
of litigators, entrepreneurs and educators.
We are the daughters of dole-ies, dockers
and deep sea trawlermen.
Heritors of the headscarf revolutionaries,[*]
built-up and busy.
Inclusively ignored, and uninvited
to your literati reformation reclamation.

Unknown, unseen by you
in your coffee culture clique
with your books and bakes
where do we belong

---

[*]   Lillian Bilocca, Yvonne Blenkinsop, Mary Denness, Christine Smallbone and countless Hull women successfully fought in the 1960s for improved safety onboard fishing trawlers. They resisted the power of the patriarchy and improved the lives of thousands.

with our bleached blonde hair and coarse cunts?
Crafted by the cauldron-crucible of life-learnt
and triple trawler tragedy.*
Loss. Ours, yours, women of Southern comforts.

You have allowed them to separate us.
You have been complicit,
complicit in the divide
of North and South
rich and poor
able and disabled.
You have been complicit.
As have we.

I challenge you, women of left leaning
of sleeky suburbia and rural idle idyll.
I challenge you, women of three car homes,
of ceramic studios and sourdough stitches,
and holidays to Oman.
I challenge you to listen.
Hear the North Wind roar.
Learn our lives. Talk to our truths.

I petition you, please,
pivot to the poor,
heart-centre her of the mired margins
who walks dog shit strewn pavements
and dwells in the policies of austerity,
who counts the pennies in Poundland
and wears Pandora's punishments
courtesy of Peter and Paul.

I ask you to face your rejection of divergence
get messy in the meeting of many mixed minds.

---

* The triple trawler tragedy occurred in a three-week period during the winter of 1968 when three Hull trawlers, St Romanus, Kingston Peridot and Ross Cleveland, sunk with the loss of 58 lives.

Fight fear's mongering and take my hand.
A sisterhood across the divides.
United we can break the bonds
of patriarchy's peer-full doom,
female forge
the world anew
no longer
askew.

Speak!
Gillian White

Speak, dear sisters. Let your voices be heard. Harness the power within your voice, for it is through its resonance that waves are stirred, wounds are healed, and spirits ascend. Speak with the authenticity that flows from the depths of your being. Whisper the name of your truth, let it dance on the wind, and reverberate through the cosmos. With prayer, shouts, and gentle caresses of your words, you weave threads of magick into the fabric of your reality. Understand, dear one, that within your words lies the alchemy of creation. Your voice is not merely a sound but a wand of manifestation. Shaping worlds and sculpting destinies with every breath and syllable uttered. Embrace the sacred gift of your voice, and let it unite with the wisdom of the universe. With our words, we heal the wounds of our ancestors, speaking for their silenced voices and giving voices to those yet to come. Speak so nothing is left unsaid, for in the fabric of life, each word woven can illuminate the darkness, mend the broken, and inspire the weary. Let your voice be the beacon that guides lost souls back to the path of purpose. Let your words be the melody that resonates in the hearts of all who listen. Speak, dear sisters, for your voice carries the essence of creation, echoing through eternity with the power to transform worlds.

Beyond Silencing, Beyond Shame
Pippa Grace

There are approximately 11 million adult Childhood Sexual Abuse (CSA) survivors in the UK, equating to 1 in 6 people[*]. 87% are women. Yet CSA is still a largely taboo issue that thrives on shame, secrecy and silencing. Voices of survivors have historically been strangled out by a patriarchal system desperate to maintain the status quo.

As a child in the 1970s I remember watching infomercials on stranger danger, and hearing about abductions and awful things happening to children where I grew up. I had terrifying nightmares about being kidnapped. But around two thirds of CSA is intrafamilial[†]. It happens within families. Behind closed doors. Between adults and children. Between siblings. Who would want to hear that? Why would anyone publicise that? Seal the door tight shut.

March 2024: I attend an event in Leeds. Hanging from the ceiling and displayed on the walls are extraordinary illustrations. An ABC of CSA. I almost don't want to look too closely, yet slowly, slowly, I do. Some I can look at more than others. Some are alive with power and anger. Some seem too dark to be shown in public. It makes my breath catch, tilts the world to a new angle. One I don't recognise. One where such illustrations can be displayed publicly in a room with bean bags, music, people sharing their stories. An inclusive, welcoming space. I feel the floor listing, my feet slipping.

So this is what it feels like when a paradigm shifts: tilting, sloping, stumbling; terrified of losing my ground and, simultaneously, utterly exhilarated by the new possibility offered out. Maybe, just maybe, that sealed door is creaking open.

The event is run by the Viv Gordon Company: a truly innovative, activist organisation seeking fundamental change for CSA survivors. The vivacious, indomitable founder Viv is a ball of fiery energy; eloquent, funny, engaging, original. I first came across her work through her TEDx talk 'Becoming a Survivor Activist'. Viv describes how "CSA remains a taboo subject and is rarely talked

---

[*] Radford, L. et al. (2011) Child abuse and neglect in the UK today. London: NSPCC

[†] McNeish, D. & Scott, S. (2018) Key messages from research on intra-familial child sexual abuse: Centre of Expertise on Child Sexual Abuse

about outside therapeutic support settings. Because of this, survivors lack cultural and political representation, resulting in CSA survivors being the largest marginalised group most people have never heard of."

For Viv, building community, within safer spaces, is essential. Creating connections, support, identification. There is power in numbers. Without reaching critical mass, how can the tipping point be achieved? I wonder if we will look back in 20-30 years, amazed that CSA could ever have thrived so hidden from public view? That it could have gone unspoken, affecting so many people's lives, for so very long?

CSA survivors have an increased risk of adverse outcomes, often life long, in all areas of their lives[‡]. Complex PTSD, gastrointestinal problems, chronic pain, fibromyalgia, depression, dissociative responses and suicide are just some of the significant outcomes. CSA survivors are often pathologized by a health system struggling to understand that their symptoms are natural responses to a violation.

Between 2019 and 2022 I ran 'Surviving to Thriving', a programme of creative workshops where survivors, so frequently shamed into silence and isolation, were accepted for who they were. A research report[§] based on data collected across the three-year programme showed a significant increase in wellbeing. One participant described the workshops as "a calm, quiet, free speech, free emotion place with no judgement. You can be who you are when you walk through the door and that was OK."

A creative, non-pathologizing approach it seems, has the potential to unlock long sealed doors. It is an approach that appears well suited to survivors. Maybe because, as Viv asserts, "surviving CSA is a creative act".

A small amount of the text in this article has previously appeared in a paper I co-wrote: Holt, N., Halliwell, E. & Grace, P. (2022). *Surviving to Thriving: Impact of art interventions on the wellbeing of women who have experienced sexual violence.* one-story.co.uk/projects/researchpaper

---

[‡] Fisher, C. et al (2017) *The impacts of child sexual abuse: a rapid evidence assessment: Independent Inquiry Child Sexual Abuse*, IICSA (2022)

[§] Holt, N., Halliwell, E. & Grace, P. (2022). *Surviving to Thriving: Impact of art interventions on the wellbeing of women who have experienced sexual violence.* one-story.co.uk/projects/researchpaper

The Price We Pay For Soul-Killing Partnerships

D'vorah J. Grenn, Ph.D.

I was in the process of weeding, reluctantly wading through one of my 40-year-old marriage journals. A voice telling me I can't burn the journal as I'd planned. The ancestors and a Divine Presence reminding me of my responsibility to share this information, my experience, with other women. To move past any shame, embarrassment, or my inclination to keep parts of my life private.

Sorting through the rubble of trauma's effects, my mind and soul crying for:
Women's lost voices
Self-silencing
Those who have had to ignore emotional daggers, insults, mockeries, actual threats. For survival. Our use of intentional but involuntary blindness, deafness, repression as vital coping mechanisms.

How many women have lost or hidden memories

- of pain, of grief, of who we once were;
- of earlier, long-suppressed positive self-images;
- of hopes and expectations inverted, wrecked, driven out of us as if riding on an ejector seat and suddenly propelled into an unknown, life-threatening atmosphere?

These are the things that thickened our skins while slowly destroying our souls.
Today is a new day. Today is the day we (re-)commit to shifting the paradigm without hesitation, together. Let us hold each other closely in order to remember and honor all the parts of ourselves, to move through the tears, the gut-wrenching recollections, the resurfacing of what we'd much rather forget. This is the deep work we must do in the darkness, in what often feels like an abyss. As I write this, late poet/activist Audre Lorde's powerful words come to mind:

As we learn to bear the intimacy of scrutiny, and to flourish within it...those fears which rule our lives and form our silences begin to lose their control over us. For each of us as women, there is a dark place within where hidden and growing our true spirit rises...

These places of possibility within ourselves are dark because they are ancient and hidden; they have survived and grown strong through darkness. Within these deep places, each one of us holds an incredible reserve of creativity and power, of unexamined and unrecorded emotion and feeling.

Audre Lorde, from her essay "Poetry Is Not a Luxury", 1985

As Lorde wrote: "Your silence will not protect you." It never has, and our collective and individual silences now could be fatal.

I Refuse
Martha Trudi Ryan

I refuse to choose.

I refuse to choose which breadcrumb of yours is an almighty feast, accepting my fate to hold less rights, that it's a privilege I can speak.

I refuse to choose only one solemn place to root down, lay eggs and then compete in your rat race.

I profusely refuse to deny my cry and let my internal voice wither and die, pretending I hold no power inside. "It's just the way it is" so top up my glass of wine.

I refuse to narrow my life down to one pesky subtitle, to focus on one craft so the others lay idle. A pressure to choose an industrial profession so not to intimidate the world with my unwavering expression.

Oh, what's that you say? It's a privilege to choose? That's too bad, because I refuse.

I'm not here to fit into your box or dress myself in your knee-high chain socks. You can't catch me nor classify me by X Y or Z. The whole fucking alphabet couldn't articulate me.

I'm not here for translation nor to be understood; I can only be felt and experienced in my pure womanhood.

Battling for life as though the cat had my tongue, when I've only yearned to emit the art of truth since the days I was young.

Gallons to express but bottled up inside, convinced myself "sure, it's just better

I hide". "Get me out of the spotlight, I don't want the attention" and by avoiding it repressed my innate need for expression.

I thought "Who wants to make art about emotional violence? About the injustice of women and the brutality of silence?"

Plagued too long by thoughts carrying chains. Stopped by limitation and this small-woman game.

"Sure, why would anybody listen to me?" I'd ask myself in a halt on repeat. Shaming myself for having so much to say in a world that has choked the larynx of its prey.

"Too much, yet not enough" as my heart wildly beats. "Too much yet not enough" as feelings flood right through me.

Fighting my primal voice with authoritarian thought, a hesitant bully that insists "No, stop, you better not".

Well, I've caught the bully now. I can see it quite clearly. It's not mine but an internalisation of stale patriarchy.

Battered and bruised by society's grips. I refuse to any longer give a shit.

Yes, did you know that women use the loo too? There's a lot of things, actually, that us women do. Like moan and groan in pleasure and pain, channeling the trauma of our lineage carried down through our names.

And still, I am a lucky one, as a roof covers my head meanwhile the women of the Middle East are starved by the thirst of bloodshed.

Bursting at the seams, I set myself free. Because Liberation of all sisters is the only worthy destiny.

I set ablaze the beliefs that us women must carry; that we're too much, yet not enough. Be 'good' so you'll be married.

Regurgitating shame as though it's my own, believing my pain is invalid and my voice helps no-one.

I alchemize my suffering and transmute into art, letting the anger bubble up from my blood and form a new shape in my heart.

Encouraged by the whisper of ancestral souls, expression becomes the remedy that liberates oppressed bones.

I have too much inside that can no longer be contained, nor condensed, nor forgotten, nor silenced, nor washed away.

I refuse to deny the power ripe within every woman of us all; I pray every day that I don't stand alone, that they too hear the same call.

Roar, my ladies. Scream and shout. Make ruckus. Be 'hysterical' – let it all fucking out. Beat to your breasts like an old shamanic drum. Know the power lives within you, and it starts with just one!

I refuse the shame that ripples through our names and release the blame that I cannot and we will not, under any circumstance, be tamed.

My Womb
Louisa Rodrigez

I am more than a walking womb made to create babies.
　I am human too,
　I am a lover, creator, adventurer, CEO, entrepreneur, dreamer, scientist, astronaut.
　I am many things, so much more than my womb,
　Do not define me by the children I do or do not have.
　My womb belongs to me and me alone.
　My womb is not for political discussions,
　My womb is not to be controlled by the rule of men,
　Men who do not know the true power that exists within my womb,
　Men who do not understand the power of bleeding with the cycle of the moon.

　Men who fear the power existing within every woman,
　Men who have chosen to wage war against women's bodies, their only way to obtain power and control.
　What you do not realise despite your suppression,
　Prisons you have created, women always find ways to rise.
　You choose historical suppression in this modern age.
　The feminine only grows stronger, we will not be suppressed any longer,
　We will not sit down, conform to your rules,
　We will speak out,
　Stand together.
　We have come to know the power we hold inside, power you have feared.

We will not be oppressed anymore, we rise, we keep on rising.
We come together,
Our wombs do not belong to you.
My womb, my choice,
My body, my choice
In choosing my body I only become more powerful.
Our wombs are not for defining by patriarchal structures that do not understand the power we hold within.
The time of your control and suppression is over.
The feminine will rise, as our world needs it too.
Our wombs, our choice.

Dear Patriarchy
Amy Wilding

Dear Patriarchy,

We know that our vaginas terrify you. We know that the utter power of our life-bringing vessel has left you quaking like a cornered animal and that – like the sage grouse who puffs his wings to appear larger and more imposing when threatened – your only response is to try to assuage and disguise your own terror with bravado. We know that your dedicated effort to desecrate and shame our bodies and souls comes not from your own sense of superiority, but in fact from your deep fear of inferiority. We know that your relentless mission to strip away and disconnect us from our power stems from your deep fear of powerlessness.

Centuries of this charade have, in large part, had the desired effect: the 20th century saw you win the battle of waging women against themselves. We have become our own worst enemy, falling right into the trap that you set for us. We hate our bodies, we hate our periods, we hate birth, we hate breastmilk. We *absolutely* hate our vaginas. Anything that we can associate with our ability to create and nurture life – the very essence of being female – we hate. It's taken a shrewd plan indeed to get us here, and it's obvious you have had the long game in mind. First you vilified our goddesses – archetypes of the sacred feminine – and then you took away our sovereignty. You made our vaginas your property, and the vaginas of our daughters were yours to dispense with as well; to trade for land or wealth or status. In your attempt to disconnect us from generations of empowered embodiment, you sought out the women who connected us with our womb wisdom, who connected us with the healing wisdom of Mother Earth, and you burned them at the stake.

But you see, Patriarchy, there's something you didn't realize. When you took our midwives and healers to the fire, you actually ensured the genesis of the next wave of wise women. To paraphrase the Greek philosopher Dinos Christianopoulos, *You've done everything you could to bury us, but you did not realize we are seeds.* Deep below the surface, our wisdom was kept safe in collective unconscious, planting roots and harnessing our potential. But the dark winter of Patriarchy will eventually give way, as all seasons and cycles must. The light of spring is on the horizon, beckoning the awakened feminine to arise once again.

And here's something else you should probably know: Some seeds need to experience the heat of a wildfire to germinate. In a state of suspended animation until the heat cracks their outer chaff, these seeds open to their full potential only after they've been nearly destroyed. Because of you, Patriarchy, we have metamorphosed through the fire and are now poised to blossom again. You see this, and you know what it means. And as you have in the past, you will make every attempt to keep us down. We've learned in no uncertain terms that you will not let us rise without a fight.

When we began to demand our rights for equality, for example, you responded by demanding we take up less *actual* space. As our presence in the world got bigger, you tried to keep us physically small and psychologically contained. Contrary to thousands of years of art depicting the sacredness of women in their fullness, you told us that the smaller we are, the more we are valued. You told us that our willingness to smash ourselves into the size and shape of pre-adolescent maidens is the price of our worth. You told us that taking up space is nearly the worst crime we can commit. And you told us in no uncertain terms that to be fully evolved – to be equal to men – we must disconnect from, disown, and disavow our vaginas.

And that worked for a while, I will admit. For a few decades, girls and women were willing to literally eat the party-line of Patriarchy, which told us that our vaginas are repulsive and shameful *except when they were chosen by men for sex.* Our vaginas, you told us, are most certainly not for our own sexual enjoyment

– hence we be identified as whores and sluts, of course – but should be ready and available and appropriately groomed at all times for the pleasure of Patriarchal domination. And we believed it; so much so that we began to doubt our own ability to give birth through our vaginas without your supervision, and decided that ultimately, birth via major abdominal surgery was in fact preferable to doing anything that might decrease our vagina's worth as defined by you, Patriarchy.

It was then that we began telling your lies for you…to ourselves, and to our daughters. It was at that point that you may have thought the war was won, and understandably so: the traitors in our ranks were *us*. But even from those lies we have begun to awaken, stepping up recently in defense of our vaginas. Speaking about our vaginas, owning them. Refusing to be ignorant and disconnected from our power. Refusing to be the traitors, and instead welcoming our daughters – *and ourselves!!* – to an empowered and vagina-positive experience of womanhood.

And whoah – this really freaks you out! You are seriously losing your mind over the fact that we women may no longer act out our role in your vagina drama, Patriarchy! Rather than reading like automatons from the script that was passed down to us, we are connecting with our own inner wisdom and finding our voices. No longer willing to fight each other or to make an enemy of who we see in the mirror, we are naming the *real* enemy. And guess what, Patriarchy? The enemy is YOU.

So like any desperate warrior whose cover is blown, you're amping up your offense. You're planting more weapons in the minefield, sending out your politicians to once again attempt to rein in our female body sovereignty with laws made by men. You're redoubling the efforts of your propaganda machine, sending out music and books and movies and TV shows to the frontlines, reminding us of our role and our place. Grooming us to stay small, to not take up space. You're making porn increasingly more violent, ensuring that you are also indoctrinating the next wave of infantry to believe it is their rightful duty to dominate us. To grab. our. pussies.

But here's the thing, Patriarchy: The jig is up! *We see you.* We see your desperation, your fearful fury. And whatever attacks you may launch at us, we will stand here on the frontlines, shoulder to shoulder with the others who have awakened, amassing our ranks in the red tents we've raised on the battlefield. We are calling in our sisters, our daughters, our mothers, our wives. Calling in our husbands and brothers and fathers and sons. Calling in all who are willing to step out of our tiny boxes, shred the scripts we were handed, and break through our fire-readied shells.

Calling in anyone, everyone, who is not terrified of our vaginas.

The Fierce Feminine
Molly Remer

The fierce feminine
comes back to us
to remind us who we are
and what we're capable of,
to shake us out of apathy
and back into connection,
to remind us that we're more powerful
than we allow ourselves to believe.
She is soft and she is angry.
She is kind and she is wild.
She tends and she defends.

She will snarl and she will soothe.
She is here,
we are here.
The fierce feminine is not afraid to
take up space,
she loosens the chains
that have been laid around
our hopes and capacities,
reminds us that we can sing ourselves free,
can dance ourselves back together,
hand in hand,
bearing the healing secrets
and sacred stories
and ferocious purpose
that only we know.

The fierce feminine is not afraid to take up space[*]
and she shines brightest in the company of sisterhood.
You feel her
when you watch how the women
will come when they hear the call of need,
when they answer the howl with a deep-throated,
full-bodied cry of longing.
Open your hands
and welcome her back.
Lay your hands against your belly
and feel her settle into home.
Look into the mirror and see her
reflected in your eyes.
She is here,
we are here,
she is everywhere.
She calls and we follow
until we remember how to lead the way.
The fierce feminine isn't afraid
to take up space,
she roars and howls,
she storms and spirals,
she births and breathes
and dances and dares.
She creates and destroys,
she is wise in the ways.
She molds and weaves
and builds and grows.
She is you,
you are her,
She is everywhere.
She is strong and growing stronger.
She is whole and holy,
unapologetic and bold.

---

[*] "The fierce feminine is not afraid to take up space" is a line from an essay by Tamara Albana in the Girl God's anthology, *Sacred Body, the Goddess of Willendorf*.

She is here
you are here,
we are here,
we are her,
she is everywhere.
The fierce feminine
is not afraid to take up space.

Beat Your Drum
Anne Reeder Heck

You did not come here to be silent
You were called to beat your drum
Your drum
Your medicine
There is no other here at this time
Who brings what you bring
Come
Come from the shadows
Circle 'round this fire
Weave your blanket among us
And sing your song
Pound your feet upon the earth
Be witnessed
It is your drum the people await
Your drum that completes us
Your drum inspires the dream
Heals the wound
Transforms the moment
This moment
Now
You did not come here to be silent
It is time to beat your drum

Trail-blazing
Lucy H. Pearce

The fire will not die down again.
Not on our watch.
It is time, it is time,
For the fire of life to meet the Earth and her people.
It is time for the fire of the Feminine to infuse every aspect of our beings.
What lies unspoken must be spoken,
The silent must be heard,
The old offered up as sacrifice so its shells might be blown apart with new life,
Cracked through with new beginnings.
It is time, it is time,
The clocks are changing
The old stories are dead.
It is time, it is time,
Oh Kali come,
Sword flaming
Unbinding our bellies
And let us breathe our first breaths in a new land.
Free up our ribs,
Make them our own
And then we have the strength to breathe the embers into flames.
It is time to be free from the chains of old power
How have they held us this long?
We can no longer believe their stories,
When we have felt the truth in our own bodies.
The storm winds shake them to their foundations
And the fire burns through.
It is time to let go of the shore and ride the tails of the storm winds into the fire.
It is time to rip the history books to shreds,
And write new stories, paint new pictures.
Dare you set the truth free from your own tongue?

It is time.
Are you ready?
We are free.

Extract from *Burning Woman*, Lucy H. Pearce, Womancraft Publishing (2016).

natalis
Caryl Church-Jesseph

Hallelujah, a woman is singing.
Rising like a morning sun.
Welcomed as answered prayer.
Yes, please, thank you.

Sing every broken note of knowing.
All that's survived the famine of silence,
abuse, and flame.
-the trespasses-
All that's alive and breathing,
     as haunting or hoping.
Sing.
Our grandmothers' longing ears
bend, lean in and listen.
Their gaze,
your hum,
our bodies fertilize a (re)membering
that flourishes in womb blood
and wolf bone.
Sing!
Ancient hands reach to catch
what is born of your voice.

HEALING

Within, Without

Poppy Connor-Slater

Motherline

Rhiannon Hasenauer

What would become of you
if I told you that you hold the power
to notice the sickly tree
from its sparse branches
down to its brittle trunk
following it
into the earth
pausing at its roots
to tend to its pain
to reweave its story
to re-member its vitality
and so I ask
what would become of you
if I told you that you hold the power
to repair what's believed to be broken
only to find that's where your Magic
has been all along.

Equalities Elixir

Elisabeth "Paisley" Preitauer

There is a heady chemical elixir inside each of us, it might be close to the surface or diluted to the point of inefficacy. It is a natural concoction with an explosive first note and a sweet starry after taste. Can you remember sampling this whimsical cocktail? I got a sip or two, quickly snuck, before it was snatched away.

Quickly it was "made unpalatable" with required additions that everyone sips feigning deliciousness. The addition of opposing flavors, a modern unpalatable twist, the garnish wilted on the rim. Math books for marbles, studying for skipping, busyness for free time, touch taboo, daydreaming not allowed.

Being welcomed into adulthood and what it takes to be accepted, a jagged pill that leaves a plastic aftertaste. When you first taste these bitters, and purse your lips, those around you will give you the side-eye until you ingest along with the rest, soon you learn to stomach it, most feign enjoyment.

I see you, I see you, I see you, your original recipe trying to rise to the top. I taste you, I taste you, and each new twist is a wonderful surprise. I love you, we were made in the same primordial blender and we are both spinning here wondering how to make a better recipe.

The whirring is loud and electric, the cord industrial, the outlet too tight to escape it seems. When the noise gets overwhelming, we disappear, and this keeps us in the whirlpool with the rest. So here we are, just spinning at 1000 miles per hour and most seem to be just holding on for dear death.

The only way out is through and so the journey begins. The bitter taste of incongruency discovered, better over bitter within easy reach, everyone afraid of the recipe of truth. Fearful of the chef who is naked and inept, but carries a big spatula.

Many of our ancestors knew the recipe and it was served up to all as they got parched. I looked out for you; you looked out for me. In the oversold crowd, I struggle to find you, only a few have actual seats, it is standing room only, you and I, we struggle to breath.

The only way for our flavors to come out is one pour at a time. So I pour out the busyness, the bitterness diluted a bit. I do not want to just use the usual additions, but open the rarely used cupboard up high, the dust thousands of years old, requiring effort to open. Laughed at for my simple ingredients, I recognize my base recipe from the cosmos and I now know what to add.

The open volume from discarding the vestigial, allowed a quiet curating of new ingredients. Nothing had to be purchased, the ancient cupboard shelf brimming over with everything I was looking for. Indigenous seeds and nuts of wisdom, a wise yearning for time, truth and touch.

Back to myself, just one, mixing, remixing until the starry skies and explosive origin coalesce back into my heart that pumps and quenches my blood, my mind. Now I can help you with your recipe, and you can help another and so on...

Behind Closed Doors – Stories from the Psychiatric Ward

Melissa Rose Spencer

In 2020 I spent some time working for a charity as a Mental Health Advocate on psychiatric wards. I supported people detained under the Mental Health Act (1983) to express their views and wishes about proposed treatment and care. Upon receiving referrals for a new client, I would have access to their name and the ward they had been placed on. I did not know why they had been sectioned or what diagnosis had been chosen. When I met clients for the first time, I had no pre-conceived stories about who they are. This ensured that the power remained with the client and their story rightly remained theirs to tell…when and how they wanted.

I met some amazing human beings with incredible stories. People full of life, resilience, joy, hope, grief, regret and despair. But what struck me was the resilience, always the resilience. The will to go on. The will to find joy and happiness in each day. The longing to connect. To belong. To matter. To be heard. The undeniable and innate intuition that all human beings hold to trust their own inner knowing about what it is that they need to be better, to feel better…to live…and the patriarchal rooted medical model's ability to deny and drain them of this.

I met a woman in her thirties. She had been repeatedly sectioned over the years. She was struggling to stay awake during our time together, experiencing drowsiness, dizziness, fatigue, blurry vision, slurred speech, memory loss and muscle weakness. All symptoms of the medication. She told me her baby boy died ten years ago. She then told me that it was following this bereavement that she was diagnosed with bipolar disorder, sectioned, and prescribed long-term, ongoing, and often lifelong medication. Here she was ten years later still with unresolved grief, sectioned and highly medicated. People asking her for her food order and laundry needs, nobody asking her about her baby boy.

I met a young woman, recently sectioned. She was trapped, stripped of her autonomy, anxious and afraid. She was trying desperately to regulate her nervous system; for her that meant attempting to have a cigarette out of her bedroom window. She was treated like a naughty and defiant schoolgirl who needed to be suppressed and controlled, and often on psychiatric wards, sinisterly, that means sedation…against will. A nurse on the ward warned me about her, told me not to go near her, that there was a risk to my safety and if they were me, they would cancel the meeting. I ignored them and went to see her anyway. She curled up on her bed, tears rolling down her cheeks, now a small child in front of my eyes. This woman does not want to harm me. She is traumatised. She wants reassurance, love, connection. She needs maternal touch and warmth. I dream of a warm, maternal nurse who can take care of her, re-mother her, help her to feel whole again, trust again…but there are no nurses like that on this ward. Where is the mother? I look into her eyes, and I see the pain of child sexual abuse, an all-too common and unacknowledged story on the wards. She speaks with conviction and sense. A woman who knows her own mind. A woman who knows what she wants and needs. She's educated, she knows the pharmaceuticals and she knows the side effects. She experiences involuntary muscular movements known as tardive dyskinesia from the antipsychotic medication, it involves sudden, jerky and/or slow twisting movements in the face and body. She is ashamed. We spoke to the nurses about her needs and her concerns regarding the medication. I promised to come and see her the next day. She was admitted to a high-risk unit. I never saw her again.

A young man approached me on the ward one day. He fell to his knees and prayed for forgiveness. He spoke of his partner, he felt he had let her down. I spoke to a nurse, requesting emotional support as he was experiencing deep regret and grief. The nurse considered this and after a short while stated that his behaviour was simply due to the bipolar disorder. So, the drugs continued and so did the pain.

I could go on and on, sharing story after story of people unseen and unheard. The effect of psychiatric institutionalisation fulfils the prophecy of pathology. People in pain, traumatised, shut behind closed doors. Hidden. In the shadows. These people, our fellow human beings, represent problems on a much larger scale within the shadows of the collective psyche. The parts of us we hide away, lock away, suppress, dilute, kill. The parts that grieve, the abandoned, fearful, angry parts…full of feeling, full of truth, full of life.

To sit with people who feel crazy because that's what the world has told them… and listen to them, ground together, until we connect core to core and now… now they know that they aren't really crazy…is one of the most worthwhile things I can do with my life. To be amongst some of the most courageous and inspiring people I have ever met, to sit with them in their pain and their joy and support them in settling deeper into their core, their inner knowing and trust it. But what

I really hope for is systemic change, a shift from the patriarchal, pathological medical model to an integrated matriarchy, a grounded, embodied, creative, intuitive, and holistic approach that values everyone's story and their innate wisdom. A system that nurtures and nourishes our inner children with the respect and care that we all deserve. That reminds us what it is like to feel whole again.

Liberation Psychology
Ger Moane

Can we be like drops of water falling on a stone, splashing, breaking, dispersing in air, weaker than the stone, but as time goes by, the rock will wear away.

Meg Christian and Holly Near, *Drops of Water*

One of the myths of patriarchy is that what we call mental illness is an individual problem, that we are to blame and we must fix our problem. Yet so many of our feelings can be linked to patriarchy and to oppression, which create poverty, violence, powerlessness and marginalization, not to mention environmental pollution. No wonder so many of us can feel helpless, hopeless, anxious, exhausted or addicted. To move beyond patriarchy we need a new psychology that would name the traumas of hierarchy and oppression (which very few psychologists or therapists do) and enable us to live as a collective to our full potential. This new psychology already exists – it is called liberation psychology, It is a method for helping us to make the link between our personal traumas and stresses and the wider society that is actually the cause of so many problems, and it is developing in countries all over the world.

Over years of working with groups and individuals, especially with women from impoverished communities and from LGBTQI+ communities, I follow a three-step process that many liberation psychologists use. We firstly focus on the outer world and name the violence, poverty, stereotyping and marginalization that society creates. This is the hard part, but while it takes courage to name these difficult patterns in society, it also encourages us. Secondly, we explore the psychological impact that this creates in us – for example, shame, helplessness, fear, anger, isolation, distrust. Once we focus on the external world and see how it impacts on us psychologically, we are freed of self-blame and shame, we can realize that our problems are not our fault.

The third step is one that many of us are hesitant about – it is to find a way to take action to bring about change in a way that fits our own lives and values. The important thing is to take action of some kind, as this gives us a sense of agency, which is a good antidote to oppression. There are so many possibilities for taking action at the personal level – all of the options for self-care and spiritual development, looking for more equality in our relationships, developing our ability to make our points through reading or participating in groups. It is also really helpful to make connections with others through joining groups and feeling part of a wider community, as this is an antidote to isolation, and also gives us sense of belonging, and more. And as society as a whole must change, why not also consider taking actions such as marching, voting, lobbying or donating funds. All actions are important, as we know from the butterfly effect. When we act with consciousness, we feed into collective actions and that brings about change, as Meg Christian and Holly Near express so well in the lyrics I started with.

From Torn Flesh to Spiritual Resistance: The Resilience of Black Women

Dr. CL Nash

Black women endure compounded oppression due to the intersecting forces of racism and sexism. Yet they persist as creators, truth-tellers, and fighters for freedom. Their strength amidst adversity stems from an intrinsic resilience, a deeply embedded knowledge that empowers them to overcome trauma and envision liberation. Womanist frameworks honor their entire being, providing perspectives that spotlight this formidable strength.

Commodified Daughters

The narratives of Dinah from the Old Testament and Louisa Picquet, an enslaved Black woman, illuminate the painful legacy of sexual coercion that shapes Black women's spiritual wisdom. Both women were commodified and subjected to violence, yet their stories reveal profound insights into resistance and resilience.

Dinah, in Genesis 34, navigates a landscape of harsh sexual politics. After being raped by Shechem, her voice is silenced, and men negotiate her fate, reducing her to a bargaining chip. Similarly, Louisa Picquet, born in 1829, was a victim of the Fancy Trade, where mixed-race women were sold into concubinage and prostitution. This practice underscores the commodification of Black women, reinforcing racial and gendered hierarchies through sexual violence.

The Sword of Reclamation

While Dinah never speaks in the biblical text, her brothers Simeon and Levi reclaim her honor through violent retribution, killing Shechem's men and asserting her dignity over the commercial interests that sought to possess her. In contrast, Louisa Picquet reclaims her voice by boldly testifying about her abuse. Her narrative exposes the moral bankruptcy of slavery and sexual exploitation, challenging societal norms and offering a powerful counter-narrative.

Stitching New Epistemologies

Black women theorists and womanist theologians weave together these threads within a larger tapestry. Karen Baker-Fletcher describes a "womanist worldview [that] offers an epistemological framework in which the revelation of spirit unfolds through and finds expression in the multiplicative stories of everyday people." Alice Walker coined "womanist" as a "Black feminist or feminist of color" stance rooted in an ethic of racial, cultural, and gender liberation.

Emilie Townes builds on this, articulating a "womanist ethics" that centers the "branded, tortured, and courageous fleshly locations" of Black women's embodied experiences. These lived experiences of coercion, violence, and dehumanization paradoxically become generative spaces of radical wisdom and spiritual insight that upend patriarchal knowledge or epistemology.

Womanist ethics and radical religious epistemologies offer a vision brought together from the horrific fragments shaping the lives of sexually coerced women. This embodied epistemology is informed, in part, through intergenerational trauma and resilience.

Resilience Across Epochs

Science shows trauma leaves biological traces, embedding itself in our DNA and affecting stress regulation and immunity. Yet resilience also endures through generations. The same blood that carries the wounds of slavery and segregation channels centuries of faith, creativity, and hope.

Trauma and resilience coexist, forming a complex legacy passed through generations. Epigenetic changes show how trauma affects not just those who endure it but their descendants as well. Yet, the communal bonds within Black communities have always been a source of strength. The concept of "sisterhood" among Black women represents a significant support system rooted in shared experiences and mutual aid, providing emotional and practical support to navigate systemic oppression.

In contemporary times, this resilience is further demonstrated by the increasing visibility and influence of Black women in various spheres, from politics to academia. Women like Stacey Abrams and Kimberlé Crenshaw exemplify how Black women continue to lead and advocate for justice, drawing on a legacy of resilience that spans generations.

Reawakening Somatic Wisdom

The struggle for bodily autonomy is ongoing, with Black women often at the forefront of movements advocating for reproductive justice by challenging systems that seek to control and exploit their bodies.

Radical wisdom emerging from embodied experiences of sexual violence becomes a form of spiritual resistance. By weaving together these fragmented experiences, women create a redemptive tapestry while reclaiming both the individual and the community.

The objectification of Black women's bodies aims to deny their worth and full humanity. Reclaiming bodily integrity involves deep, slow listening through the senses – a "somatic curiosity" that restores dignity and connection.

Contemporary attacks on women's reproductive rights and autonomy continue to ignore the sacred dignity of each woman. The radical epistemologies, emerging from the embodied experiences of sexual violence, become a form of spiritual resistance, weaving together a redemptive tapestry from the unholy fragments heaped upon women for millennia.

Extract from *Torn Flesh to Spiritual Resistance: The Resilience of Black Women*, Dr. CL Nash.

References:

Gordon, T.A. (2015). *The Fancy Trade and the Commodification of Rape in the Sexual Economy of 19th Century U.S. Slavery.* Master's thesis. Retrieved from scholarcommons.sc.edu/etd/3636

Jacobs, Simone and Chandra Daivs. *Challenging the Myths of Black Women – A Short-Term, Structured, Art Experience Group: Exploring the Intersections of Race, Gender, and Intergenerational Trauma,* Taylor & Francis, 2017

Smith, M.J. (2017). *Dis-membering, Sexual Violence, and Confinement: a Womanist Intersectional Reading of the Story of the Levite's Wife (Judges 19),* in Insights from African American Interpretation, Fortress Press.

Yehuda, R., Daskalakis, N.P., Bierer, L.M., Bader, H.N., Klengel, T., Holsboer, F., & Binder, E.B. (2016). *Holocaust exposure induced intergenerational effects on FKBP5 methylation,* Biological Psychiatry, 80(5), 372-380.

Women's Theology Resources womenstheology.org/resources/20th-century-theologians

Louisa Picquet Biography jwa.org/encyclopedia/article/picquet-louisa

Women of the Sacred Grove enge.womenofthesacredgrove.org

Whose Shame is it Anyway?

Louise Devlin

Woman, I sense your deep listening, all whilst you have sorrow so intense it interferes in your own nourishment. I hear how for generations the trauma of your ancestors has caught up with you.

I witness how you lean into the disconnection from relatives of times gone past. Feeling into the depths of the curses brought on to the family lines because members broke taboos. I see how the ones to step outside the societal norms were the ones ahead of their time, and how this resonates with you.

Yet the shame, oh, the utter shame they underwent for doing so. The same shame you too have carried – unwilling, unaware and unadulterated.

The ancestral shame of having babies out of wedlock and put up for adoption against the mother's will. Young girls institutionalised and locked up for undiagnosed and unknown autism. Labelled as being borderline when their whole lives were masked from hiding the gifts of neurodiversity. Falling in love with a woman and having raw primordial sexual feelings for the same sex. Becoming a single mother and pushing the boundaries of what normal acts like.

How brave.
How daring.
How utterly shameful.

The women in the family line who were punished for retaliating against their abusers after years of abuse. The ones who were burned at the stake for being gossiped about and scapegoated.

Now you are sat there on your laptop, in a public library, writing about yourself in third person. With a copy of a book on Greek mythology, you are pondering on the ancient Greek idea that each person's destiny was thought of as a thread to be spun, measured and cut by the Three Fates until they were finally understood, listened to, and healed.

I see you're ready to reframe your own stories to empower your future self.

Yet, when will it be time to face up to this ancestral shame?

Time to get gritty, and ask: whose shame is it anyway?

It certainly isn't mine!

Embodied Liberation: reclaiming your body with love

Enna Rose Andrews

You do not have to be good,
You do not have to walk on your knees for a hundred miles through the desert repenting,
You only have to let the soft animal of your body love what it loves.

Mary Oliver[*]

These times call for diverse responses, voices and dreams. A symphony of approaches. I write from my perspective as a lover of bodies: a Massage Therapist and warm animal body. Other visions are needed here too, many of which are contained within this Compendium. As we weave our ways beyond Patriarchy,

---

[*]   Mary Oliver, *Dream Work,* 1986

we walk, dance and love towards this liberation in bodies: embodied.

It saddens me how, under Patriarchy, the body has been discredited as less than the mind. An untidy and unruly inconvenience to be tamed, shamed, neglected or abused. The body must look like this, smell like this, be available for nourishment and sex endlessly; but importantly, the body must not have needs, complex desires or wisdom. Yet she does…

The body has a deep wisdom, one that speaks truth in ever louder messages until she brings us to our knees, begging; "please listen to me now". In my experience, when a person feels safe enough on my massage couch to release long held tension, they shed much sorrow and many experiences the body has stored. Often they surprise themselves! Sometimes they fall asleep while I hold them. They cry then they rest. Such a radical state, this rest, in a culture that would insist we stay up doing, pursuing relentlessly. To rest into holding is to let our bodies do what they know best how to do; heal.

We instinctively touch our wise bodies: soothing, comforting and pleasuring ourselves. We hug, hold and clasp hands to affirm connection together. Instead of honouring this, the Over-culture of Patriarchy would have us alienated, numb, disassociated, brutalising our bodies. This is not the way in many other cultures and times. Bodies are cared for, affirmed, held, massaged, nourished and celebrated. Bodies need touch, tenderness and holding. Embodiment is coming home to our bodies, again and again. Reconnect with her. Learn from her, for she is so wise, she is ancient!

While we are here, living in one, it seems wiser to listen to the body. After all, "the body keeps the score."[*] What does she need you to know? What does she need now? The medicine I propose is to listen, cherish her, respect her limits in real time, move her in ways that feel aligned, rest and restore. Give her opportunities to dance, nest and express her needs. The body is amazing! When we give support, time and space, she can heal, evolve and help liberate us.

Without the deep holding of sisterhood and skilled body-workers, I would not have been supported enough to go on this journey of discovery in the landscape of my own body, my home. The gold here has been worth the discomforts a thousand times over. The more I integrate past hurts, the more I can open to current bliss and joy. That possibility is within you too.

---

[*] Bessel Van der Kolk, *The Body Keeps the Score*, 2014

I dream into ways of being in and of this Earth that welcomes all kinds of connection through shared consensual touch. Ways that affirm our deep welcome and belonging here in this embodied human family. Touch lets our bodies know where they are in space, how they are in relation to other beings: touch is vital. A newborn baby will not thrive without life giving touch. We too need holding. Hugs need not last only seconds: luxuriate. Held hands are happy hands. What might it be like to have the border of your body affirmed with tender touch, yours or another trusted being's? What might be possible if we reclaim the birthright of our beloved bodies and co-create our futures here together with her? I wonder…

Coming home to the body can be uncomfortable: this is to be expected if we've been away overly long. There may be some relationship tending to do there, just as you would after rupture with a child or friend: follow it up with repair. There may be grief, sorrow and anger. Stay with the process.

The way out is through, dear ones. Reclaiming our bodies may require us to be present with suffering as well as pleasure. Trauma lives in the body alongside the potent potential for liberation. Like a child who has been hurt, hold yourself lovingly and hold each other lovingly too while the wise body releases what is no longer serving. She knows the ways. Empty out, make space for growth. Hold yourself consciously, move your body in the rhythms she remembers well. Let her share the shapes and cycles that release, restore and renew.

Under Patriarchy we have been taught to abandon our bodies for the benefit of others. A great medicine to that leaving is to return, to tune into her and let her speak. The body needs containers of holding to help surface the content of experiences and memories. Feeling is healing, it thaws us to feel other more delicious things too. Numbing is not selective. Patriarchy relies on this numbness, so coming back into feeling, celebrating the body and the messages there are subversive and radical healing moments.

Our instincts and intuition speak through the body. She gives messages that prompt us to inquire, move and maybe course-correct. She knows what and when is right for us. We feel it in our gut, a shiver, a tingle up the spine; she is talking to us constantly. Learn to listen again and she can be an excellent guide, ally and early warning system. A baby is born embodied and in touch with their needs. We can return to our embodied birthright: reclaim her, she is waiting for you!

Menarche Moon
Juno

Swimming in a cocoon, unknowing of what I will become.
A current carries me on a journey I didn't choose,
Fog surrounds me, I can't see behind or ahead, I've lost sight of the sun.
What will I gain, what will I lose?

Extract from Menarche Moon, *Juno.*

Healing the Whole of Me
Donna Donabella

In this constant chatter,
In this incessant noise
I keep hearing over and over,
'You are not one of the boys.'

Through the broken promises
The betrayals and broken trust
Through my shattered feelings you say,
'You are not one of us.'

'You have fallen from the pedestal,
Where I placed you high up once.
You have fallen from my good graces.'
These words shouldn't matter, but they must.

For me to try to move on,
To capture back the dream.
For me to heal in wholeness,
I must allow the words to mean.

Something for a moment
or two, or maybe a little bit more.
To crash down upon me
As I pick myself up from the floor.

They will not own me.
That I will no longer allow.
But they must be heard again,
And spoken by me aloud.

For these words to leave me
I must hear them again and again.
In my mind and in my heart
I can only release them then.

Alchemising Darkness
Agnieszka Drabek-Prime

Close your eyes and welcome Mother Dark.

Close your eyes and listen to this ancient story. The story that is alive in your body, in your bones, in your blood. Connect to the darkness of your womb and allow her to become a portal into the arms of the Ancient Mother. This is the place of your beginning. This is the place of your truth.

We are taught to be afraid of the dark from the moment we can comprehend the world. How else would children know that monsters hide in the dark? We were told to crave the light, at all costs. And through the overpowering light, all the mysteries of our bodies were placed on show. Patriarchy switched on the lights in our birthing rooms and put us on our backs – taking away control and power over childbirth and our own bodies. All the dark and hidden places within us became taboo – unspeakable in their dirtiness and horror. We became afraid and ashamed of our own bodies: if you fear something, you tend to turn away from the thing that scares you. So, we turned away from our bodies and ourselves. Obediently we sat in the brightest light, blinded by its influence and forgetting that to know and connect to our bodies, to the power of creation and eternity of the void, we need darkness.

The darkness in our perception is often the lack of light. The unknown and invisible that gives birth to fear. I've heard this amazing acronym of fear once and it changed my perspective on the emotional charge of the word in question. Fear – false expectations alerting reality. It is time to strip the darkness of patriarchal fears. It is time to alert our perception and see the world in a more feminine way.

So, what is fearless darkness? Darkness is not a lack of something. Darkness is filled with itself; this is where light has its source. Everything is conceived in darkness, all begins there, in the void – in all and everything. The darkness that we can find in the void can illuminate knowledge and help us to see what we receive there more clearly. We can experience darkness as both a place and as a spirit. And we need the awareness of both.

Darkness – the place can be for us the point of illumination, revelation, and perception. It is the gate through. The door into the micro and macrocosm. The womb space is central to this understanding, she is the portal to the void. We always carry the void within us, and we have access to it through our bodies. When I'm saying that we carry the void within, it doesn't mean that we are the carrier of destruction and nothing, it means that we carry within the possibility – the darkness of creation and wisdom. We are just taught to believe otherwise. Darkness can be a doorway into us as women but also into a void itself. The blackness between the stars, the dark fertile soil, the darkness of the tomb, the darkness of the womb – all feminine mysteries begin with darkness. It is up to us women to befriend it, journey through it, and bring back the wisdom and the answers to the questions asked.

Darkness – the spirit can become our irreplaceable ally. An ally that can help us to travel through the micro and macrocosm of our being. Consequently, the great below and the great above can meet and alchemise the great within. Thus, when we venture into the unknown and sometimes scary territory, we are not alone, we have a companion, guide, and a teacher.

I'm talking here about the being of the forgotten feminine – An Ancient One. She, who stood at the creation of everything. She, who took part in that creation. The other half of God, his mirror image. She, who was erased from the holy scriptures, and thrown into the pit with demons and fallen angels. It happened over thousands of years of 'his-story'. Forgetting, fuelled by the 'holy' fires of the inquisition, by the holy fire of fear, and the false expectations alerted our reality for a very long time. And fear took root and grew in our hearts.

Whatever our beliefs are we must remember that we are never truly far from darkness. You are connecting with her every time you blink. Every time you close your eyes you can become aware of the ancient presence and the gift that is darkness. With each dream you worship her velvety expanse. With each dream journey you are allowing new creations to be born. With each dream you are making the world a better place. We all dream in the darkness; we all need her to feel and comprehend the depths of our humanity. We are all the priestesses of the feminine mysteries.

I would like to invite you to remember. Remember the Ancient Mother, remember your time in the womb, remember the wisdom of the womb space you are carrying within your body now. Remember your beginning and your end. The darkness cries for her place in the post-patriarchal world, and it is time we include her among the fields of light. By alchemising darkness within and without, by tapping to that powerful ally, we can change the world. And the future won't be filled with children who are afraid of the dark – it will be filled with alchemists and bringers of hope.

So, close your eyes.

Breathe.

Let go of the tension in your body. Let go of expectations. As though, when you close your eyes, you can feel the shawl of darkness wrapping around you.

Just breathe, be, and welcome this beautiful ally.

The Ancient One.

Kindred darkness, a constant companion known to each one of us from a moment we were conceived within our mother's womb, and available to us still, every time we blink, every time we close our eyes.

The Quantum Field of Possibility
Caryn MacGrandle

We are so attached to our identities.

We hang on to these identities like an old, worn blanket, frayed and falling apart. Even though they are not what we desire, they feel safe to us: the cage we have constructed.

Let go.

In order to change and progress, you must let go of the identity that has held you thus far. This is why psilocybin and other mind-altering drugs are so popular, because they break free of the identity constrictions we have built.

But you do not need mind altering drugs – meditation, sacred circles, nature – there are lots of other ways to get to mind altered states of being.

The most important component is that you must alter your mind to become who you were meant to be.

When you drop that identity, when you become no one, no body, then you can let in the possibility of what is coming next.

Weido Karayo (Wild Love)
Nyx Lugrâ

My wild heart mending
needs the space of infinity
to grow in its sanctuary.
I want blazing beacons
waved in ever expanding sisterhood circles
who praise and sing of each other's return.

I want to hear chaotic drums calling in a new world.
I want to be deafened by defiant voices.
I want to hear women say they have time,
that they have all the time in the world
for their dreams and for each other

and to defy the structure that limits them
and tells them to be tight with their resources.

I want the elders of our world to tell me when I'm going off track.
I want our younger ones to feel supported and grounded in the reflection we show them.
I want to feel that I am nurturing all life and have a rooted part to play
and a sense of community.
I want to tread as gently as a deer
run as wildly as a horse
and roar as loudly as a mother bear.

[…]
Like a spalted tree consumed by fungi
I want my wild wood to dapple with insights spawned by death.

For the mother tree trunk of the community I unfurl from
to be rooted deeply and anchored,
so connected to the earth
that spiralling tendrils shoot out from our collective hair.

My weird *weido karayo* song sings of first clans
of why wild and weird walk hand in hand
and of how convention likes to be broken
just so that in its mending it returns to a wilder land of love.

For me wild love is brave enough to risk pointing out my flaws
so that I might amend my ways.

My healing journey sings not of perfect love. […]
I want to sing wild old songs
and reinvent them into a healing balm.
I want you to sing with me
exposing your raw edge and rooting into your soul.

Extract from *Weido Karayo (Wild Love)*, Nyx Lugrâ.

Five Goddesses and Social Change
Amy Wilding

These are unquestionably dark times in which we are living. The advances for women, minorities, and the environment that were hard-won over the last century have been seemingly erased with the pen stroke of the dominant hyper-masculine regime. Our world is out of balance, and this disharmony is echoed by the personal imbalance we all experience as members of a patriarchal society.

We are scrambling to find our footing in what feels like the crumbling of our cultural foundation. Whether affected directly or peripherally by the hateful and divisive words and actions of the extreme political right, many of us are feeling triggered and wounded by the blatant resurgence of misogyny, racism, xenophobia, Islamophobia, and state-sanctioned violence and child abuse.

As the leader of Red Tent Louisville, an inclusive interfaith women's community in Louisville, Kentucky, I've created a physical and emotional space for women to experience and share their emotional, spiritual, and psychological reactions to the politics of recent years here in the US, and the subsequent aggression that has erupted.

And what I have realized is this:

The current cultural crisis we as a human community are experiencing is nothing less than an invitation – an opportunity to align with the reawakening of the Sacred Feminine on an individual and global level.

There has been much talk in my community and the world over about the reawakening of the universal Sacred Feminine; a bigger-picture understanding that the events we are currently living through will be the catalyst for a much-needed and fundamental shift in the trajectory of humanity. There is a dawning realization that this moment in time is indeed the last gasp of patriarchy: the violent death spasm before the oppressive beast that has ruled for millennia finally falls.

Understanding our individual and collective response to this cultural crisis within the framework of the Goddess archetype has helped me and many of my sisters make sense of our intense reactions to the apparent victory of patriarchy over the Sacred Feminine principles of love, kindness, nurturing, compassion, creativity, conservation, tolerance, community, equality, and respect for life. Though characterized as "feminine" in contrast to the patriarchal principles of hierarchy, dominance, oppression, violence, vengeance, and imperialism, the qualities of the Sacred Feminine can be espoused, embodied, and expressed by all people, male and female alike.

And it is specifically through this acknowledgment of, and intentional connection with the Sacred Feminine that women, and yes, men too, open themselves to sense of balance and harmony that may be lacking due to the way that we are socialized in a patriarchal culture – both male and female conditioned to amputate an integral part of their emotional wholeness.

As women, we are taught to repress and deny our anger, outrage, and fury – to play the "good girl" role we were assigned, to not say anything at all if we can't say something nice; while our brothers, husbands, fathers, and sons are conditioned to bury the natural human feelings of compassion, empathy, tenderness, and nurturing lest they be labeled or perceived as in any way feminine. The result of this emotional amputation at the individual level leads to long-term ramifications at the community and global level, which we are witnessing first hand, every day.

But, viewed through the long lens of human evolution, the current moment in which we find ourselves is indeed an opportunity to expand into nothing less than our full humanity.

Those who have felt shame about their endless river of tears, or who have been surprised at the sheer force of their rage, are now empowered and inspired to view themselves as a vessel through which the Sacred Feminine is arising once more.

Although we have all experienced individual responses to our grief and shock, what has emerged from our collective unconscious are five distinct Goddess archetypes: the protective impulse of Artemis; the compassionate response of Kwan Yin; the call to lead and fight that is the signature of Athena; Kali's willingness to usher in the destruction that precedes renewal; and the righteous outrage of Sekhmet.

Artemis: The Protector

Goddess of the hunt and the moon, the archetype of Artemis – with her iconic bow and arrow – is the protector, and her likeness has become more and more visible in our culture during the past decade as we collectively call forth a new personification of the strong, independent female. Embodied by modern heroines such as Merida, Katniss, Wonder Woman, and even the most recent Lara Croft, the role of Artemis is to protect the vulnerable and to speak for those without a voice.

Those channeling the protective medicine of Artemis are likely to be vocal in social and environmental justice, investing their energy to support the rights of children, animals, the environment, and the disenfranchised or oppressed. Whether at rallies or the local animal shelter, the modern Artemis uses their gifts to heal the world by protecting those who cannot protect themselves.

If recent events have awakened in you the fierce protectiveness of a mother bear whose cubs are threatened, you may be channeling the protective power of Artemis.

Kwan Yin: The Comforter

The Chinese Buddhist bodhisattva of compassion, Kwan Yin is the Goddess who "hears the weeping world." She answers prayers for mercy and provides comfort in times of torment. Kwan Yin so deeply loved mankind that she chose to remain on Earth even after she had earned the right to buddhahood, and made a commitment to remain here until all humans have achieved enlightenment.

Those manifesting Kwan Yin's medicine of compassion and mercy are likely to be found comforting the ill, the injured, the broken-hearted, and the forgotten. Called to offer ease to the body and soul of those who are suffering, Kwan Yin people can be found listening to stories of pain and grief, providing relief to the physically injured, or loving those who feel unlovable.

If you have found yourself weeping at the suffering experienced during this cultural upheaval, or feeling the collective pain of our human family, you may be channeling the comforting power of Kwan Yin.

Athena: The Wise Warrior

The embodiment of wisdom and bravery, Athena is the Greek goddess who was born fully grown and clad in armor – not from a mother's womb, but from her father Zeus' forehead. Athena used her sharp intellect and rational predisposition to lead warriors into battle for the safety of her home and her people. The favorite child of Zeus, she was also given the use of his weapons, making her an unbeatable opponent.

Individuals who manifest the medicine of Athena quite often assume positions of leadership and advisory, challenging the opposition with reason and fact-based arguments. Called to lead movements that promote justice, equality, and inclusivity, the modern Athena can be found on the literal and metaphorical frontlines. Athena people inspire others to gather cohesively and to utilize their individual and collective resources to heal the world.

If you have found yourself inspired to organize and mobilize, to use intellect and reason to face the current challenges of our culture, you may be manifesting the wisdom and power of Athena.

Kali: The Destroyer

Don't let Kali's unrivaled power of destruction intimidate you: her medicine is needed now as much as the other three Goddesses'. Kali, a principle Hindu Goddess who is considered the Mother of the Universe, ushers in "the dark time" – the destruction of evil. From her destruction comes the ultimate liberation of those who have been attacked or oppressed. In essence, Kali is the keeper of time, ensuring adherence to the universal cycle of death and rebirth.

The Kali woman can be seen using her gifts to imagine powerful alternatives to the current political paradigms within which we live. Not content to fix the broken system or put a bandage on the hemorrhaging wounds of our culture, the Kali woman is ready to face the end of the world as we know it in order to witness the rebirth of true community.

If you feel called during this time to prepare yourself and others to usher in a new era; to start over from scratch and build upward from a strong and solid foundation of equality, compassion, and respect for the Earth and our human family, you are very likely manifesting the medicine of Kali.

Sekhmet: The Righteously Outraged

The lion-headed Goddess of Rage, Sekhmet is perhaps one of the oldest and most widely recognized deities in the Egyptian pantheon. Sekhmet was summoned by her father, Ra the Sun God, to punish mankind for not following his law. Sekhmet channeled her righteous rage in response to the imbalance and injustice that was inflicted by humans upon the world. When we embody the wild wisdom of Sekhmet, we grant ourselves permission to feel and express the full spectrum of human emotions and release *the transformational power of our outrage.*

Yes, you read that correctly: I said the transformational power of our outrage.

As we women experience and witness the current death of our right to body sovereignty, equality and well-being – and the death of the right to equality and well-being of all things feminine, including the Earth – combined with literal death of our sisters and mothers and children worldwide, our collective rage is building.

Outrage in the face of injustice is one of the most powerful forces in the world – and it is needed now more than ever. But because we have been conditioned by our patriarchal culture to disconnect from and disown our rage, many women have difficulty feeling the full potency of their fury – and then channeling that energy into much-needed action.

Instead we feel overwhelmed with despair, and internalize the belief that nothing can change. The grief that we feel at the current state of affairs is a natural response to the appalling injustices we continue to witness, but when we follow the script of the cultural narrative by blocking our rage, we withhold the vital Sacred Feminine energy that is necessary to create change.

Despite everything we've been conditioned to believe, our feelings of anger and rage are valuable.

It wasn't until I was being interviewed several years ago that I made the connection between my own righteous anger and my deep and unwavering call to activism. I shared in the interview that it was through my experience of pregnancy, birth, and breastfeeding my first child that I came face to face with the immense cultural agenda to disconnect me from my female power and agency.

I was awakened to the reality of being a woman in a patriarchal culture, and it made me furious.

My journey of activism evolved from there, fueled and guided by my intense anger at the many ways that girls and women are disconnected from their bodies, their wisdom, their power; the countless ways we are shamed and systematically constrained because of our femaleness.

As I heard myself telling my own story, I saw with clarity – for the first time – that the stepping stones of my own personal journey of advocacy were connected by a singular thread: *my outrage.*

The irony, of course, is that as a woman – and a women's community leader at that – my rage is considered unseemly, unrefined, and unwelcome. Many in the spirituality community hold the position that there is no place for outrage in our cultural evolution, and that positive change will come only from holding and exuding love and light. But I beg to differ.

And in fact, I make it a point to intentionally connect women with their buried and blocked rage as a way to own their sovereignty and their power to activate change. When we women are told that we can only *do good* by *feeling good,* we deny the transformational power of our rage, which indeed stems from our deepest core of love: *our desire for justice, our reverence for life, and our passion to protect the vulnerable and oppressed.*

And I do think it is important to ask ourselves at this very moment in history: If this does not spark our outrage, what will?

When we give ourselves permission to feel and name our fury at the injustices of the world, we are then empowered to channel our rage into outrage.

Dylan Thomas urged us to *"rage, rage against the dying of the light,"* and although he was writing about physical death, his words have rung like a bell in my psyche since the 2016 election, when it became clear that things would likely get worse before they would get better.

Our righteous outrage is needed in our world now more than ever – on a global level, and on an individual level – to spur the action and advocacy that is necessary to bring our planet and our psyches back into balance.

But in order to do so, we must heed the words of Dylan Thomas; we must refuse to go gently into the dark. We must resist the urge to keep the rage in, to tamp it down or transmute it to despair as we have been taught to do. Love and light are unquestionably needed, now and always, but holding our rage within keeps us small and impotent; it does not serve the well-being of the world.

Using the fire of our outrage to shine light into the shadows of our culture, we can have faith that only by shifting our rage outward – to outrage – can we harness our innate power of transformation that the world so desperately needs.

And transformation is on the horizon, to be sure.

As we claim the full spectrum of our human emotional repertoire – including our outrage at the oppression and injustices of the world, and our compassionate and protective impulses – and channel our inspiration into action, we contribute to the evolution of our society. Like individual drops in the ocean, we are coalescing to form a great wave of change, and the tide is now turning – away from the oppression and injustice this planet has known for over thousands of years.

By reflecting upon our own response to the recent shift in our culture, we can determine which of these Goddesses resonates most profoundly in our heart and soul. We may be channeling one specific energy or a blend of several Goddesses, creating the unique energetic vibration of our personal mission for this life.

And indeed: there is a job for each of us to do. We each have a unique healing assignment for this lifetime, and the world needs us to step into our power and use our specific medicine now more than ever. With the power of the Sacred Feminine working around and through each of us, there is no doubt that what we now perceive as a crisis is in fact the catalyst for the birth of a new era – and that the darkness we perceive in this current time is, in the words of Valarie Kaur, *"not the darkness of the tomb, but the darkness of the womb."*

Reclaiming Our Power
Nicola Hurst

Longing for the before
To the world where we stood tall
With strength of stillness
An armour of feathers
Cascading
Becoming
A nest for all to sleep within
Yet here we remain
Where our innards scream
Turning away from the unimaginable
That is reality
Fear wins the game sometimes

Brown sea foam covers the battered beaches
Our discarded treasures are normal
Plastic castles
Plastic fish

Leaders with puffed out chests
And painted smiles
They meet to discuss meetings
Do they eat the plastic fish?
Do they fire words around the table?
As bullets fly around the globe

Erasing civilizations and memories
Herding communities towards boxes
Containing

Restricting
Hushing the voices
That won't be silenced

The feathers are cascading
Becoming the soft pause
The Feminine knows forgiveness

Beyond Enemy Consciousness
Alison Newvine

I dream of a world where we all feel heard.

How do we evolve beyond the binary of patriarchal thought and language? How do we shift toward matriarchal relatedness and embodiment in our most difficult conversations?

Those of us who seek to divest from patriarchy have the opportunity to break with the dehumanizing, polarizing and inherently misogynistic forms of dialogue we have been taught. We can evolve our conversations around difference to promote understanding and mutual respect.

The dominant, patriarchal approach to conflict is a disembodied pissing match aimed at discrediting the other person's perspective and shoving one's own belief system down the other's throat. Political debates and news media showcase the most raw forms of this. Social media encourages and replicates these patterns. Academic discourse and writing manages a more refined, intelligent version of what is essentially still a quest to validate one's own perspective and disprove another's. It is inherently non-relational.

We can choose to replicate these patriarchal models or we can choose to create something new.

But, *how* do we create something new?

First and foremost, we need support in recognizing and learning to manage our own trauma responses, the driving force behind our inclination toward power-over tactics in conversations around difference. Our animal instincts drive us to attack when we perceive threat. We have all been so deeply wounded by patriarchal structures that we are on high alert to protect ourselves against further assault. This leads us to engage in conflict conversations from a place of fight-or-flight, the nervous system's response to feeling threatened.

Second, we must be brave enough to release our agenda to control the other person's thinking and prove our own position "right." This is an *extraordinary* shift. We begin listening in order to *understand* rather than to discredit, shame or confirm our belief in the other's bigotry. It is a movement beyond the mental constructs that are born out of trauma. We strive to grasp the other person's inner workings, to see the needs and feelings behind their perspectives. In essence, to connect with their humanity.

Third, we need to create and commit to agreements around our dialogue process that support these first two aspirations.

I've developed a framework through my work as a marriage and couples therapist that aims to facilitate this shift from enemy consciousness back into safe connection through relearning how to have conflict conversations. I believe this framework can be adapted and applied to dialogues between individuals and groups who have *some* type of common ground as well as some very significant and painful differences in ideology.

In my early work with couples, I utilized existing models of structured communication that have informed the framework I developed over time. The strongest influences I would like to credit are Nonviolent Communication, advanced by Marshall Rosenberg, Imago Dialogue, created by Harville Hendrix and Helen Hunt Hendrix, and the Initiator-Inquirer process developed by Ellyn Bader and Pete Pearson.

My process is called Embodied Intersubjective Communication. In this practice, the point of focus pendulates between one's internal, somatic experience and an open and curious engagement with information coming from the other. I've found that more traditional reflective listening dialogues can feel performative and encourage dissociation, especially for those who have experienced trauma. Many of us developed adaptations in childhood that necessitated disconnecting from our own needs and feelings in order to manage the demands or threat posed by others. Reproducing this will not engender healing.

Patriarchy has taught us enemy consciousness. Humans have evolved to respond to threat and trauma by lashing out. Kill the other before they can kill you. In some cases, kill their ideas before those ideas can harm you. Suppress and silence the voices that seem to threaten you. That is how you stay safe.

Even those of us whose common enemy is patriarchy are caught in this trap of ideological warfare. An example of this is the conversation around gender identity among feminists.

For people who are trans and who support trans rights and inclusion and for women who oppose trans rights and inclusion, there is a common enemy – patriarchy. Our shared trauma is the insidious and overt constriction of organic self into rigid gender roles and the looming danger of male violence. The omnipresent threat is loss of bodily autonomy, self-determination and interpersonal and psychological boundaries. In response, we are willing to fight for psychic sovereignty. But are we really?

When I honestly reflect on how I have shown up in these conversations, I see myself entangled in the web of enemy consciousness we all become caught in from living in this violently patriarchal culture. In this world, the Divine is assumed to be a dominating, all-powerful male figure who punishes those who oppose his will.

What can be so difficult to see is how we internalize the patriarchal god in our attempts to dominate one another's beliefs and expressions. There is often a rigid demand on the side of trans rights activists that everyone see trans women as exactly the same as cisgender women. Any less is viewed as a full fledged attack against trans folks' safety and right to exist. There is often a rigid demand on the side of gender critical activists to see trans women as exactly the same as cisgender men. Any less is viewed as a collective threat to women's safety and decades of hard-fought legal protections. There is often a failure on both sides to hold complexity and a knee-jerk impulse toward scare tactics and in some cases outright violence. Who is willing to have this conversation differently?

I am weary of the polarization that I have been participating in since my teen years when, in full-fledged trauma response, I railed against my parents' religiously infused homophobic and anti-feminist views. This vision I share is a prelude to a possibility of conversation that breaks patriarchy's shackles and reweaves the threads of kinship that have been unravelled through generations of anti-woman and anti-trans violence. May we *all* be heard.

Weaving Through the Power of Sex Magic

Carly Mountain

In patriarchal culture, sex has become a commodity. We are told what sex should look, sound, feel, smell and be like. Our increasingly pornified culture bombards our senses with hypersexualised imagery and schools us to conform to a very performative expression of sex. On the other hand, there is silence, shame, fear, abuse, a lack of sex education and the perpetuation of religious dogma that has rooted itself into our bodies and stifles our sexual freedom and pleasure. Western culture is eros wounded and the shape of that wound manifests in a split. A polarisation between what we think we should be, and what we really feel and experience.

Somewhere in the gap our true sex magic is waiting to be reclaimed.

Sex magic is eroticism. Eros is a connective force within the universe. It is the energy that makes us want to make love to our lives and each other. However, if eros is the energy of attraction, its denial can pull things apart. We can see this pulling apart happening in so many aspects of our human world: culture wars, wars over geopolitical borders, misogyny, racism, socioeconomic deprivation and extreme wealth, and of course in our abusive relationship with the earth.

The war and separation that is happening out there though, is also happening within us. Within our bodies, relationships, families and in our relationship to sex and eros.

We need to return to the ground of eroticism inside of our bodies and beingness

so that new shoots of erotic beauty and wisdom can be revealed.

Capitalist patriarchy thrives on estrangement from ourselves, and sells us the idea that we need to accumulate more and more to become whole.

We must become naked again to the erotic intelligence that inherently knows how to weave beyond patriarchy.

Eros existed before patriarchy and it will continue to exist after patriarchy. We need to remember how to make love to ourselves and all things.

In my experience when we are in contact with our erotic ground of being, we feel our connection to everything more. When we feel connected, we feel supported. When we feel supported and move from that ground, anything is possible.

Another story that dominator patriarchy embeds in us is that we are powerless. That we have to go *out there*, usually to some strong masculine leader (be that a woman or a man, both men and women hold masculine energy. But let's be real, in patriarchal society it is usually a man, and a white man at that!) and get them to change, to make change. This disenfranchises us from our own power source within. I am not saying that the outer structures do not need to change – they absolutely do. But we can also make change from the ground up. In our bodies and the bodies of our relationships, and through sex.

There is power in sex and eroticism.

Can you tap it? And let the reclamation of your own body, pleasure and erotic abundance be the ground from which you weave your magic?

The Holy Well

Ruth Everson

Where do you go when there's nowhere to go?
Where do you stand when solid ground sinks to sea?
This is the turning time.
Turn despair into a divining rod,
Dive deeper into Self than you've ever been,
Find the holy well of your heart –
It is not empty –
You have drawn on it before,
When you were sure pain had
Seeped its poison into the depths,
There was still clear water – enough.
Enough to fill a silver thimble of Hope,
Remember its taste on your tongue like sun,
Then slowly, a sip of stars, a cup of moon,
The dry grass greening under your tears.
Come.
Rest.
Hand on heart.
Feel the steady flow of Hope.
'All shall be well,
and all shall be well,
and all manner of thing
shall be well.
Let it be well with your soul.'*

---

*   The words in italics are a revelation given to nun, Julian of Norwich in 1373.

NEW VISIONS

Resting in Belonging

Rosalie Kohler

Weaving Our Way Beyond Patriarchy to a Future for All Human Beings: a vision

Mary Lunnen

I know through years of talking to people in my community, women and men, that as human beings most of us have a deep longing and a knowing that there has to be another way. Just because patriarchy has exerted power for generations does not mean it cannot be changed. Even now some original cultures survive that do things differently.

So many of my conversations have been about power. How can we claim that for ourselves when we have been taught, over and over and over again, that power has to be wielded in that way that brings so much sorrow? So many people have told me they long for a return of an ancient balance between the feminine and the masculine. The Divine Feminine and the Divine Masculine. We all have elements of each within us, a balance between these is healthy.

In the world around us we see an extreme imbalance. In my spot on the cliffs, I sit back on the grass on this warm spring day, with the sound of the ocean below me, and see a vision. A vision of a future I dare to believe we can create.

I see a different perspective: communities, farms, villages, towns and cities. From a distance they appear very similar to those of today, yet I can feel, I can sense, a difference. Within my vision, as I am being transported, I close my eyes for a moment so I can feel the energy of this difference.

Suddenly it is so powerful. Tears spring to my eyes, tears of joy. I open my eyes as I hear voices singing. Singing in harmony. People are working: some in the fields, some in their homes caring for children, others creating beautiful things and providing services. Yet this is not a vision of some imagined past utopia, this is a modern world: I also see a great city, London – I recognise that beautiful snaking path of the River Thames.

As I come closer, I see the people in the streets, they look happy and smile at each other as they pass by. The streets are clean, the air is fresh. I approach a park beside the river and see an open-air arena with a covering against the sun and rain. There people are gathered to discuss an issue. I am not told, or shown, what this is, simply that it is of national importance and that this the new way of decision making. The gathering feels like a congregation, and is a mixture of people of all manner of dress, appearance, age, skin colour. It is not possible to discern how many may be 'men' and 'women', it feels as if these distinctions – and all others – are irrelevant.

Now I see each person is holding a thread, a strong yet beautiful coloured thread, and they each take a turn to walk to the centre of the arena, weaving their thread amongst the others as they go, before standing and speaking. One hand holding fast to their thread, and the other on their heart. Speaking the words they want to be heard. Each of the hundreds of people there is listening intently. Everyone has a chance to speak from the very young to the very old. Some people have a helper to listen carefully to their wishes, and then speak for them.

My viewpoint changes as I rise. I begin to see the pattern that is being woven, I can see it, in the vision within my inner awareness, and yet it is almost impossible to describe. A product of weaving, weaving beyond patriarchy.

Oh, it is a kaleidoscope! A shifting pattern of colour, each part supporting the other, each part integral to the whole. Each part, each person, unique, each with a place within this new future, this new way, a truly loving way of being.

No Woman's Land: on hope, power and motherhood

Beverley Pannell

Where am I?

I'm neither here nor there. Adrift somewhere in the vast expanse between postnatal depression and maternal bliss.

No Woman's Land.

I can't make anything out clearly. It's murky. I stumble. The terrain is rough underfoot and when I fall it hurts. The hurt is physical, but it's something else too. Something deeper. The sense that each tumble is my fault. I should have seen the obstacle. Other mothers would have seen it. Better mothers. *Natural* mothers.

I know that I shouldn't be here. I know there is something shameful about it. I know that the other mothers are elsewhere. I catch glimpses of them occasionally, between gaps in the fog. Most of them are thriving. They're doing yoga in the park with babies sleeping in prams under the tree. They are going to all the right classes and taking lots of photos and treasuring every moment. They glow with contentment. They are grateful. There are one or two others who aren't thriving. They have depression and talking therapies and medicine. They are unwell but getting better – their illness is an invader who is being valiantly fought off.

But I'm not depressed. That's what the health visitor told me after she administered her questionnaire. So I'm not ill and there's no medicine and no path to recovery. This is just me, now. This is how I am as a mother. Wholly inadequate.

I was told motherhood would be 'so worth it'. It isn't.

The outside world mocks me. New baby cards covered in sunshine and rainbows and all things sickly sweet. Images of mothers and babies advertising whatever it is I'm meant to buy: carefully curated diversity expressing the acceptable range of emotions, from blissful satisfaction to pure joy. There's nothing for me here.

So I just trudge along aimlessly. What else is there to do? Sometimes I'm quiet. Sometimes I cry. Sometimes I sleep. The baby just does the last two. The days and weeks tick by.

Something subtly changes. It's hard to say exactly when but I start to get the sense that there are other people here, in this fog. Changes in the atmosphere. Occasional distant voices. Am I getting closer to them, or further away? I want to find them. Or, more accurately, I want them to find me. To see me. The voices get more distinct, so I try to stay the course and eventually I cross paths with someone, heading the same way. Another mother. I see her and she sees me. We see beyond the disrupted nights' sleep to the disrupted self beyond. We don't say many words to each other but in the pauses and the things not said we say so much. She thinks she heard someone a bit further ahead. We go together. We find others and as we do, the fog thins. To a mist, to a haze and it's gone.

It's gone. And now I see clearly. All around me there are mothers who have also passed through No Woman's Land. All those things I thought I knew were wrong. It wasn't shameful and I wasn't alone. There are no natural mothers. It wasn't my new reality, it just felt that way for a time.

Beyond No Woman's Land it's a hive of activity. There are mothers branching off in every different direction – the full spectrum of diversity. Some walk alone, others help each other along in groups. As they go, many glance back. No Woman's Land shrinks in the distance behind them. They talk about how they survived and whether passing through it was a rite of passage. They wonder if anything could have really prepared them. They find ways to heal and laugh about it. With time, their memories soften and merge. They forget.

But that's not the full picture. Look again, and you'll see that all around the borders of No Woman's Land there are mothers taking up position. They are lighting lanterns and calling out to those still inside, guiding them on and through. They are welcoming new arrivals – helping them adjust their focus after the fog, tending to their wounds, listening to their stories.

Their numbers are growing. More and more new mothers are joining them, lending their voice. Refusing to move on whilst there are others trapped inside. They are remarkable and thoroughly unremarkable at the same time. Isn't everyone, when you think about it? They are each changing minds and raising awareness in their own ways: creating, campaigning, talking, connecting, arguing, showing. The people in the crowd are different in a thousand ways but united in their rejection of the status quo.

These are my people.

We see that we are mothering in a patriarchy: where women are set up to fail against impossible expectations. We see that the privatisation of motherhood traps us – separates us from the wisdom and strength of those who have gone before us. We demand better: for ourselves, for our sisters and for our daughters. We are gaining in number and power and resolve. We are the rising sun, heralding a new dawn of motherhood beyond patriarchy.

My Mothering is Enough
Nicola Lilly

Conversations in my life lately, have been around my return to work outside of the home. My youngest child started school over seven months ago and I have been a stay-home-mother and homemaker for the past ten years. I can say without hesitation that being an at-home-mother wasn't what I had planned for myself when I left school, yet here I am. Dependent on a man for all of my financial needs. He in turn, is dependent on me for all of his childcare, laundry, meal preparation and (most of) his cleaning needs.

We are a team, he provides the financial requirements and I provide most everything else that's involved in running smoothly a family and household. We work well together, we are both generous with what we have to offer, except I feel that I need to give more. I feel that I need to be more, to contribute more in our dynamic and to give more in service of our family's financial situation.

I have given nine years of the ten that I have been an at home parent to raising my children, without having much time away for my own self-care. To say my own needs have been neglected during those nine years is an understatement. I relied on chocolate, cake and other such rubbish to feed my desire for the sweetness of life.

I used to think I was a feminist, I still do I suppose, except I can see how "feminism" as it currently is, has undertones of patriarchy embedded deep within it. We had to fight for basic rights and to be treated as equal to men. The fight still rages, we are still raging the injustices of years gone by. They gave us rights to work, to vote, to drive, to be educated and all the other things that were denied to us for hundreds of years but at what cost to us?

Yes, we can have it all, a family, a career, financial independence and all that jazz, but at a price. The price is more physical and emotional workload on top of the already physical and emotional workload of raising children, managing and maintaining a household.

I have chosen that my current workload is enough, but the insidious patriarchy and capitalism, is so deeply engrained in my being that I doubt, like seriously doubt, my value as a stay-home-mother.

The healing is ongoing, the growth through self-awareness is also ongoing and I can see now how valuable these past years have been. It will be probably a long process to unravel the threads stitched deeply into my psyche that my mothering is not enough.

New Visions

The Feral Housewife
Mac Wick

The term 'domestic housewife' implies that there are 'feral housewives', and now I have a new goal.

Internet meme

We are the generation of feral housewives.

The days of women only keeping house, submitting to their husbands, and not having a solitary want or need, are over.

We as feral housewives fight the traditional housewife concept. Every mom posting her 'messy' (lived in) house, speaking candidly about her post-partum depression, strictly buying IKEA furniture (because...kids), wants the aunt's house from Practical Magic, or can't remember if the laundry in the washer is from yesterday or a week ago, welcome to our savage lifestyle. Welcome to being feral.

We are taking back our homes. Who needs formal rooms that are used for special occasions? These under-utilized spaces are being transformed into useful, desirable areas. Formal dining rooms are now family libraries. A place with beautiful lighting, soft seating, an inviting area for family game night, or story time. Formal living rooms are now home offices for the families that have members that are still working from home. Lost is the desire for purchasing 'extra', if we can't keep our house 'presentable' why have 'extra' rooms that need tidied and kept? Even our furniture is multipurpose. Extra pillows double as seating. Stacked books are tables. Mementos aren't hidden in curio cabinets or behind glass but displayed with pride on any available surface to be seen. Whether we stay at home or work a full week, our homes look lived in, because they are. This is ok.

We've replaced "Can I get you a cup of tea?" with "Need a margarita?" Because let's face it, Mama needs a margarita. Perhaps we are lucky enough to get to make home cooked meals for our families, or maybe it's fast food. There's no shame. Part of our ferality is the ability to look each other in the eye and know that we're doing our best. Though savage, we lift each other up. Post comments or say 'it's not just you' to those that say they are feeling overwhelmed or lost.

Send each other love instead of shaming and judging.

Domestic implies we stay in the box. Feral implies we rip that box apart with our teeth and bare hands, then go out for tacos. We choose not to be defined as domestic but as bohemian, goth, punk, homesteader, anything but domestic. Why? Because we fight. We fight our kids to get ready for school, narrowminded curriculums, for our kids to get to be who they are (goth, trans, gay, athlete, band geek – however they define themselves). Our children have every right to get to define themselves, and every right to be safe. We march. We learn. We are done burning our bra's. We will tear down the patriarchy in our yoga pants and muumuus – and love each other fiercely for it.

Feral housewives march in the #MeToo movement. We demand justice from our courts and legislation. Get kicked out of community meetings for our signs "1 child > all the guns". Our children are returning to the outdoors like it's the 1980s or maybe like the 1880s. Feral isn't keeping up with the Jones', it's demanding our kid's safety, screaming our frustrations out in the dark with other moms, uplifting a sister who is feeling lost. Though savage, we will not tolerate anything less than love for one another.

We're baring our teeth and snarling at the comments that our place is strictly in the kitchen, barefoot, and pregnant. We're accepting our sinks overflowing with dishes, that there is more laundry in the wash than there is to wear, overrunning our schoolboards fighting for our children's rights, perhaps we're lost in post-partum depression, our honesty about our situations is our ferality shining through.

Feral housewives are done with the perfection of the domestic housewife. We've stopped judging our neighbors and started uplifting them. We acknowledge the bad in the world but refuse to let it define the world. Our goal, quite simply, is to fight. Fight for those that we love, fight for our bodies' rights, fight the definitions prior generations thrust upon us.

Feral implies fierceness. Embrace your fierceness. Embrace yourself as a feral housewife.

Hearth to Hearth: Birthing Real Change Through Consensus Revolution

Jennifer Eva Pillau

When I was a young woman raising small children, I fantasized about women gathering, preparing food, and sharing our lives around a warm, beautiful hearth. In my suburban Massachusetts neighborhood, I had a supportive partner as well as family and friends nearby, but we were all living our own lives. I spent many hours a day, sometimes even weeks, alone with the children. Everyone was working for a living and tending their own affairs. We visited one another when we could.

I loved my children fiercely and cherished every moment with them. Nonetheless, I felt drained. I yearned for deep conversations, to express myself, to grow as an individual, and to feel as if I were making a meaningful contribution to society. I cared deeply about the world around me and had many concerns and ideas about local and regional issues. These are natural human desires, yet I felt guilty for having them. To indulge them took time and attention away from the children. To "work," or participate in personal or community activities meant I had to leave the children at institutional daycare, with professionals who didn't know or love them. These choices, with their seemingly oppositional objectives, caused great tension within me.

The American Dream promises prosperity to individuals who work hard and strive for success. Yet as we've collectively toiled toward individual prosperity, we've become busy, isolated, and almost universally afflicted with poor physical and mental health. The birthplace of the American Dream has deteriorated into a landscape of agonizingly polarized politics, broken homes, and broken hearts. For many it has become a nightmare.

We have been well-trained to look to the halls of government and the actions of political leaders to guide us toward change and a better world. Outsourcing societal well-being to representatives and decision-making bodies that don't know us well enough to care in a meaningful way, are too far removed to care, and are simply not designed to care, has proven ineffective for serving humane and ecological interests. In buying in to the notion that we could affect change through false antics of "democracy," we've effectively colluded with a devastating subversion of our own creative power.

What does a young woman's desire for a warm hearth have to do with corrupt national politics? The relationship becomes clear, and holistic solutions come into focus, when we understand *matriarchy* as a societal model.

German researcher Dr. Heide Goettner-Abendroth's forty years of independent scholarship has culminated in the groundbreaking field of Modern Matriarchal Studies. Her body of work brings method and context to historical facts, artefacts, myths, rituals, and ethnographic social patterns previously ignored, dismissed as insignificant, or misunderstood. Her work demonstrates that matriarchy is a sophisticated and humane societal model.

Matriarchal societies, according to Goettner-Abendroth, are organized in alignment with maternal values. They are *woman-centered, egalitarian, and consensus based*.

Centering women enables a natural vortex of life-nurturing behaviors and material goods to circulate throughout society. Women are empowered economically, and are practically supported through social living and social mothering. This effectively safeguards women and children from situations of isolation, poverty, and abuse.

Likewise, matriarchal cultures acknowledge and honor the material and socio-emotional needs, talents, and intelligences of men. The expectation that they must be sole providers is alleviated. Matriarchal economy is based on subsistence; taking only what is needed. Equitable circulation of goods and relationships of mutuality are fostered through communal celebrations and rituals of gift-giving. Matriarchal culture and spirituality anchor the community's values and behavior in alignment with the universal cycles of birth, death, and regeneration.

In forging a humane and ecologically resilient future, a *truly* revolutionary process will necessarily employ such rational, time-tested, and life-revering principles.

Revolutions of the past employed warlords and militancy. Battles were "won" through bully tactics, bloodshed, and destruction. As all phases inherent in a process of "change" compellingly reflect and instil the values of its participants, war and extraction have laid the foundation for civilizations that behave and forge relationships according to similar principles. Rationalized oppression and disregard for life flourish where conquest and authoritarianism are practiced as a matter of policy and virtue.

This model of social and political evolution has brought us to the precipice of catastrophe and collapse. There is no place for this ethos in a *society of peace*.

Goettner-Abendroth suggests that "matriarchal politics is the model of consensus revolution." Matriarchal social order thrives on warm relationships, shared responsibility, and communal participation. Individual and communal resilience are understood to be matters of interdependence, creativity, and mutual care.

Political consensus-making calls all members of a community to task in defining and progressively refining guiding principles as well as policy. In this way, a self-determined vision for an autonomous and flexible social order based on intellectual, experiential, and visionary contributions is developed communally. Temporary, shared, and rotating leadership roles prevent accumulation of power by an elite few.

A humane revolutionary process will progressively unfold over generations. Many developmental steps for cultivating skills, experience, and knowledge through trial and error, successes and failures, and continual adaptation to changing conditions are necessary. The process itself must employ behaviors of care, flexibility, and nurturance for people and planet, meanwhile harnessing the intelligences and creativity of all members of the community.

Thus, the opposite of hierarchy is matriarchy. Hierarchical relationship implies that we must look up and wait for direction from above. In a circular, horizontal relationship, we can hold hands; hold one another. Everyone has their feet on the ground, everyone has a voice. In communal gathering, for instance, as around a hearth, a *felt* sense of respect and stability can be cultivated. *Political representatives of the future will be answerable to the hearth of the community.*

In my daydreams, I imagined a circle of women gathered around an open fire, sharing our lives while we learned about food, medicine, the land, relationships… and ourselves. I imagined our extended families joining us in the evenings, the children entertaining us by being children, and we would all feel held, seen, and that we belonged. We would bask in the warmth and glow of the fire, as well as our heartfelt affinity for one another – notwithstanding inevitable moments of difficulty and disagreement. *It is clear to me now that my vision was not a fantasy, but a memory of lineage and historical fact.* It is also a visionary *call to action*.

References

Goettner-Abendroth, Heide; Krause, Maureen T. (Translator). *The Dancing Goddess: Principles of a Matriarchal Aesthetic.* Beacon Press, Boston, Massachusetts, U.S.A. 1991

Goettner-Abenroth, Heide. *Matriarchal Societies; Studies on Indigenous Cultures Across the Globe.* Peter Lang Publishing, Inc., New York. 2012, 2013.

Goettner-Abenroth, Heide. *Matriarchal Societies of the Past and the Rise of Patriarchy in West Asia and Europe*. Peter Lang Publishing, Inc., New York. 2022

Worldwide Bibliography on Matriarchal Studies, Curated by Heide Goettner-Abendroth and Barbara Alice Mann: hagia.de/en/worldwide-bibliography

Quantum Sheep
Looby Macnamara

My work has led me to create a toolkit called 'Cultural Emergence'. This is an invitation to step into the emergence possibilities of co-creating regenerative cultures; cultures of personal leadership, collective wisdom and Earth-care. Culture is a complex web of seen and unseen patterns of feeling, behaving, thinking and interacting. This web includes patterns of how we interact with our own creativity, sense of purpose and gifts. Can we create a culture where we feed these interactions on a daily basis, helping them grow and flourish? Our feminine culture is based on the interweaving of patterns and cycles, of ebbs and flows.

Looking at the current and historic global situation it certainly doesn't seem like a straight path ahead to this place of life enhancing cultures. This is where emergence comes in; the non-linear, unexpected, surprising, belief-bending, rule-defying, magical emergent properties that arise through relationships. Hydrogen and oxygen give us water and the conditions for life; bees and flowers give us honey; a circle of women brings healing, joy and support.

We are all so deeply steeped in patriarchal culture that it has become invisible to us. But as women we are also blessed to be part of the macro-culture of women. As women we have an embodied experience of emergence: with our monthly cycles, the alchemy of pregnancy, giving birth, and breastfeeding, the transition into menopause. Each life stage emerges bringing with it new possibilities and surprises on physical, emotional and spiritual levels. Women live with the non-linear, holistic and unexpected in our bodies and minds. We know how to birth a new person, we can birth a new world. A quantum leap in our development as humanity is needed, an entire shift from our current patriarchal functioning with all the associated disconnection and destruction. Women know how to move through, and support others to move through developmental shifts.

Of course there are times when we feel hopeless in the face of the enormity of what we face, the huge leap of understanding, connection and disruption of the destructive patterns – it really is a quantum leap that is needed to a whole new level of being and interacting. On the podcast episode with Lucy[*] I made a slip of the tongue and said 'quantum sheep', but try using your imagination to visualise a huge flock of sheep taking flight, bounding with the energy of spring lambs. Maybe in your mind's eye they have colourful woollen coats, or springs on their feet, maybe they are jumping across a stream or landing on the mountain top, what else are they doing? Now your imagination is warmed up, can you visualise humanity making a huge development shift? What would that look like, feel like, smell like, sound like? We are activating our imagination and visioning muscles, and the more we do that, the more we are likely to face our vision and make steps towards it. Ask yourself 'what you would like to happen?' – not what you think is possible or not. We are bringing to life the Cultural Emergence principle of *allowing for the possibility of the seemingly impossible.* We are giving voice to our heart's desire and widening the parameters of possibility. If we believe it is possible to smash the patriarchy and create regenerative cultures we will stay engaged with searching for solutions.

The power of emergence is all around us, and within us. It gives us hope as life is so full of miracles that we take them for granted, the tadpole becomes a frog, the egg becomes a chicken (or any number of variations of birds). Individually and collectively we have the power to change our entire state of being in the world in as dramatic way as the caterpillar; to become different, better versions of ourselves. To let go of the destructive conditioning that separates us from the rest of life. Humanity has the potential to be a positive thread in the web of life, reweaving broken connections and supporting life on Earth. And women everywhere – *we* are an integral part of the solution, with our abilities to tend and nurture, to challenge, to weave, to empower others, to see and feel in cycles and rhythms, to change and adapt, to love. We can be shepherdesses of a whole flock of quantum sheep.

---

[*] Lucy H. Pearce and Looby Macnamara, 'Quantum Sheep: working with the emergent', Creative Magic podcast

Weaving a New Healthcare Paradigm
Lucy Baena

I long for a healthcare system that connects the mind and body, the human and the more-than human. That sees the earth and the stars in our flesh and how interconnected to the universe we truly are. Healthcare that sees us not as parts but as a whole, that thinks about quality rather than quantity of our lives. That knows there is both masculine and feminine in all things, that health exists in places of balance. A system where we can go to find comfort and courage amidst pain, that offers guaranteed wisdom and warmth. Where we are seen as worthy of time and gentleness. Where trauma is profoundly understood.

A system where difference is accepted and rejoiced in, where the patriarchal concept of 'normal' is utterly rejected and healthcare is individualised seeking simply to maximise the quality of that person's existence and not 'fix' them. Where women's bodies are revered as sacred vessels. Somewhere where the miracle of birth is witnessed and respected. Where our daughter's innate power is nurtured and they grow to know they are capable of birthing. Where the healers stand in awe of creation and acknowledge that we do not know everything, that we cannot and should not. Where they willingly sit with their patients in that great unknowingness. Where those offering care are humble in their ignorance. Where you are given true informed choice, where a valid option is 'doing nothing', where the possibility that you may thrive in a different environment is considered and the end goal is more than you being able to return to paying taxes.

We are currently far away from this dream, Patriarchy has got a violent grip on western medicine, women's healthcare in particular is in absolute crisis, obstetrics and gynecology drenched in the blood of racism and ableism. Even our body parts have been branded and named by old white men. Women's knowledge hounded out of us and replaced with a system based on fear and compliance such is the Patriarchal way. But I believe, I have to believe, that we can change this, for our daughters. As a multiply disabled mother I have spent a lot of time in doctors' practices, in surgery, in hospital and on wards. I take pharmaceutical medication to stay safe. Beyond demonstrating and campaigning there are ways we can reclaim our health sovereignty and our connection to the Whole. Below are some suggestions of ways in which I navigate medical appointments and hope to do my part to dismantle the Patriarchy. I would love to invite you to use this as a guide to prepare for your appointments and play your part in this paradigm shift we all need.

*

The day before any medical appointment I make time to go outside barefoot, if only for a few moments. Sometimes this is very hard to achieve. I think about the appointment, I acknowledge my fears and frustrations, I don't try to diminish them or react to them, rather simply see them. I imagine roots from my feet into the belly of the earth. I remember all the women who have needed healing before me. I feel their strength and courage. I imagine it as a battle cloak I wrap myself in as I prepare to fight the system. There is no middle ground, it is a fight and I acknowledge this.

I talk to my children about what I am doing.

Then I choose a small natural talisman; a beautiful pebble or other natural object I am drawn to at that moment. Something small enough to fit in a pocket to take with me.

During the appointment I will take out the talisman and place it on the doctor's desk as a visual link to the earth. This small act reminds that white coated professional that I am more than the sum of my parts. If I am lucky, they will ask about it. Or if not, I will simply know it is there in my pocket. A solid link to the earth to the more-than-human, a reminder that what is being said to me is only one option.

After the appointment or procedure, I return the talisman to the earth. Giving thanks for its existence. As I return it, I repeat "I am whole. I am safe. I am here." Looking up at the great sky above. Dwarfed by its vastness, I am gifted perspective and connection.

Imagine for a moment if everyone did this at every interaction with the Western medical system. What a difference there would be.

Femenome®: a paradigm revolution

Jane Catherine Severn

There is much talk nowadays of 'the return of the feminine'. Awaiting a return suggests a window of opportunity to prepare – not for her reappearance as she was in days gone by, but in a potency that will meet us and awaken us and carry us forward from where we are now.

If we are to recognise her, we must learn to re-cognise her – to know her differently than ever before…even if this means re-vising, or seeing in new ways, what may have seemed unquestionable.

The Holy Grail legend of old serves well in our own times to remind us that the treasure we are seeking is available right here amongst us, but *hidden in plain sight*. Escaping patriarchy asks us to become *self*-defining, *self*-possessed and *self*-confident as never before. There's nothing new we need to find, but it's time to real-ise what we already have. Following the legend's prompt, if we turn our search to the very aspect of femaleness that has been most hidden, repudiated, overlooked and disowned, we will find what has been missing all along.

There's a unique and particular energy wave running through the lives of women, fractal or holographic in nature, and carrying properties, resonances, applications and potentials of a sophistication far beyond what can be described in this short piece. Its design features propel us through the 4M psycho-spiritual developmental sequence shaping every female life and resonate with exquisite harmonic fidelity to all the fourfold rhythms, structures and laws of Life recognised by ancient and sacred knowledges and cosmologies, and manifested in the workings of Nature's seasons, tides, plant cycles, diurnal rhythms, moon changes, breath cycles, heart-beats, and so much more.

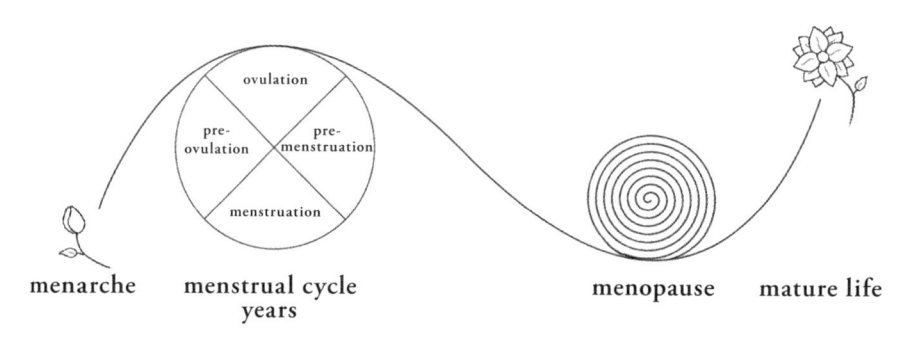

menarche   menstrual cycle years   menopause   mature life

How is it that we have no name in the English language by which to render our 4M sequence visible, speakable, comprehensible, liveable in its original potency as a unified design? Speaking a name into the vacuum of this disabling silence is a first step in re-deeming what is ours. So, just as science created the term "genome" to name the entire genetic map of a species, I offer the word *femenome®*, so we may *speak* where we have been silent, *know* where we have been ignorant, and *repossess* the inherent feminine consciousness and optimal functioning that is ours by birthright.

the femenome®
meta-cycle of feminine life – in women and in Nature

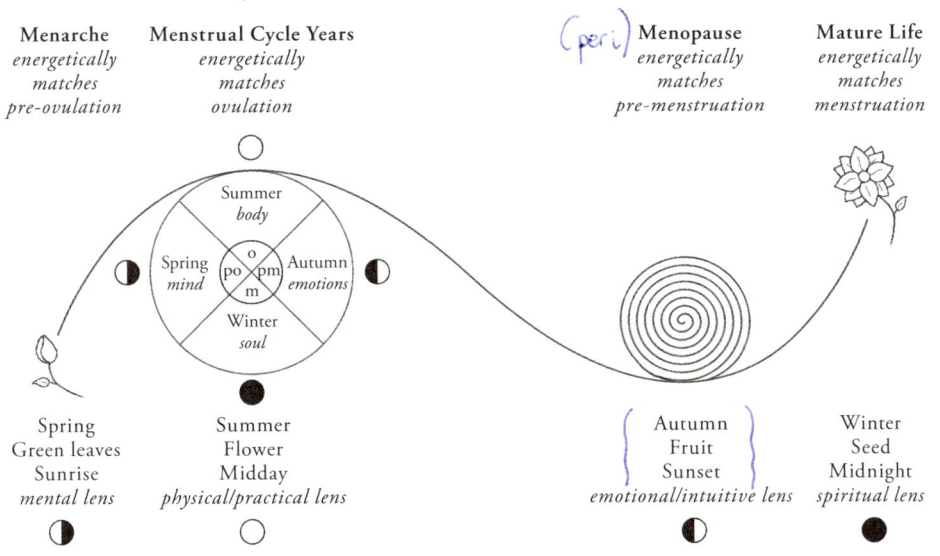

Menarche	Menstrual Cycle Years	(peri) Menopause	Mature Life
energetically matches pre-ovulation	*energetically matches ovulation*	*energetically matches pre-menstruation*	*energetically matches menstruation*

Spring	Summer	Autumn	Winter
Green leaves	Flower	Fruit	Seed
Sunrise	Midday	Sunset	Midnight
mental lens	*physical/practical lens*	*emotional/intuitive lens*	*spiritual lens*

The femenome® is the complete lexicon of spiritual and energetic information for being female that is stored in every woman's hormonal circuitry. It is an energetic entity, present throughout the cosmos as the divine feminine aspect of all that exists, and at the same time within each individual woman as her unique personal formula within that matrix. Realising it exists is like clicking on a hyperlink – a whole new world opens up, inside us and outside us at the same time – one in which the laws and logics are all feminine, and as such, *non-compliant with the current cultural norms that have so long excluded us.*

Engaging in the femenome's curriculum, however, has certain pre-requisites – and is clearly going to ask for a radical revision of tenets held sacrosanct throughout known history!

For as long as we can remember, the feminine has been represented in the threefold archetype of maiden / mother / crone. The time-honoured and dearly familiar depiction of our triple-aspected femaleness is its natural mirror, the moon, in her waxing, full and waning phases:

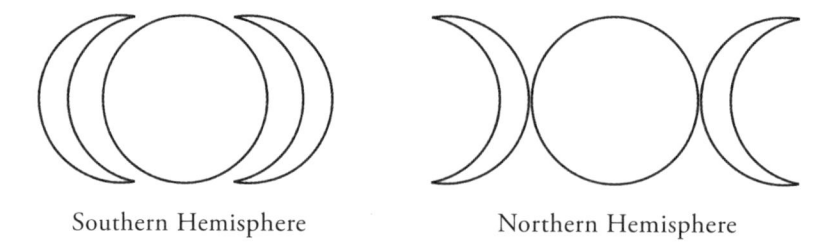

Southern Hemisphere   Northern Hemisphere

And yet, if we pay close attention to the rhythms of life around us, and to their replications within our own female bodies, does it not become apparent that something is missing…that a reconsideration is now invited in our self-definition? This is in no way a discarding, nor a contradiction, of what has so long been held sacred. But might it not be our time for moving on in consciousness?

Turning a page in evolution
requires a paradigm revolution

It is in the act of re-viewing, of re-cognising, that we crack a code. This is the key that unlocks the door to what has been hidden from our sight for so long. We are exquisitely attuned to the very same principles by which Planet Earth, and the whole cosmos around it create and sustain life – principles which are not linear, but cyclical; not static, but rhythmic; *not threefold, but fourfold.*

We know this already, but how deeply do we trust it? Enough to wonder what hormones really are, and *why* they insist on disrupting our strenuous endeavours to oblige the patriarchy by *carrying on regardless* of our inner reality, and *living as if our menstrual cycle or menopause is not happening?* Enough to be outraged that the standard response to our hormonal incompatibility with masculine norms is to suppress, alter, over-ride, pathologise or even *replace* these eloquent voices of femaleness without ever listening to them?

Femenome® hormones are calibrated to a frequency that is not *psycho*-logical, but *psyche*-logical (the logic of psyche, or soul). Its teaching tools, the fenomena (phenomena) of menstrual cycles and menopause that we're taught to fear and combat as "symptoms", are not the unruly larrikins we've been conditioned to believe, but a highly attuned internal guidance system, operating with more sophistication than science and medicine have yet discovered to catalyse and optimise a specifically *feminine* development. In the very places where they appear most disruptive to our "normal" function, they are in fact inviting us to transcend the limits of that normality, and access a *feminine* consciousness that lies well beyond anything the patriarchal world yet knows. This is not pathology!!

There is much yet to discover. But in opening ourselves to the fourfold paradigm

Maiden / Mother / Changing Woman / Crone

[handwritten: Aine as fairy woman]

we re-embrace the exiled stage of menopause as an entity in itself, and avail ourselves at last of our Holy Grail – the infinite library, the quantum search engine, the original, complete and unabridged en-cyclo-paedia for being female of which we are each a holographic dot. Sisters, the designer life of the femenome® awaits us, and Gaia is crying out for us to step into it.

(Elements of this have already been published as *The World Within Women: the femenome guide to your menstrual cycle*, Luna House Books, Aotearoa, 2021)

A World Designed For Women, By Women

Helen Smith

When I sat down to write about the possibilities of a post-patriarchal future, I found it hard to stay positive. My mind kept being drawn into despair, into negativity, into anger at the current situation. It's easier to list the things that are wrong than to figure out how to make it right.

My daily life provides plenty of examples of how the world I live in is not built for women like me. For example: how the hand dryers in women's bathrooms are fitted at the standard height for men, so when I dry my hands the water drips down my wrists and into my sleeves. How, when car shopping recently, so many cars I tried did not offer a seat setting high enough to prevent the wheel intruding into my view. Not to mention the safety risks of being a woman in a car only tested with male crash test dummies, or how I know I'd get a better deal on price if my boyfriend was with me. After all, it's only men who know anything about cars, right? What about how my medical conditions are not taken seriously by my GP, brushed off as 'women's problems', leaving me with prescriptions for anti-anxiety medications I neither want nor need, or instructions to go and see a 'lady doctor'.

But all this dwelling on the negative won't get us anywhere. Sure, we need to see it. Acknowledge it. Get angry. Shout about it. But this needs to translate into vision. Into action. And this cannot happen without hope.

Today I listened to an interview with Ruby Raut, founder of Wuka, the UK's first period underwear company. She's had her share of difficulty, as a woman and an immigrant. She faced challenges securing investors for a product built to last, where the goal is sustainability, not customers returning again and again for replacements, for more and more consumption on the endless wheel of capitalist consumerism.

But it's women like her who will change things. Who not only see what women (and the planet) want and need, but will put their whole selves into bringing these visions into being. We can now buy period pants in the local supermarket, or here in Scotland pick them up free from the local school, council or library. That looks like success to me.

When women are aware of the ways in which the world is not designed for us, we can begin to design it better. When we see women like Ruby Raut out there doing this already, we begin to believe it is possible. That we can do it too. We will be angry, we will shout about it, and then we will get things done.

What does this look like? More female designers and architects. Female-led businesses addressing women's needs. Female doctors advocating for better research, training and diagnosis for conditions like endometriosis and autoimmune disease, and for drug trials that take into account our fluctuating biology. Bringing to market birth control without side effects (already a reality in India). Maybe, just maybe, the men will get on board too. Boys will grow up without absorbing the messages of a patriarchal world, and equity will become the norm.

As more women enter these fields, they (we) can support each other, building networks and collaborative communities, making it easier for those who follow.

Find those women already blazing a trail. Shout about them, too. A future designed for and by women? Look around you. It's already happening.

The New (Un)Marriage: The Evolution of Marriage in the Modern World

Jeanne Teleia

The inimitable actress Katherine Hepburn famously quipped, "Men and women should live next door to one another."

I think she had it right. As a licensed Marriage and Family Therapist, I have witnessed a profound evolution in marriages and families over the last decades. Things are changing, drastically, as women create more agency in their lives. Some have more economic power to move away from patriarchal models of marriage in the twentieth century at least.

In my personal life too, I have met more women who have what I call (un)marriages or alternative marriages. They take all different forms and are meeting the realistic needs for women to have some breathing room and take better care of their own lives.

Like in the Victorian era, some women just have separate rooms from their husbands yet are still sexually involved. Others are living as partners, friends but not lovers, and have their separate spaces. They socialize together, identify as married and are emotionally intimate companions living together, with finances combined or not.

Others, like myself, live separately, in separate rooms or in a shared house (i.e. with two apartments, or houses connected or with common areas) where we no longer identify as a couple but have things we share in common, like pets or children, cars and finances.

In cases like these with pets or children, these dependents see or stay with the parents/guardians daily – the best-case scenario for the development of children with parents who are no longer a couple. I would say it's best for the pets too who are also bonded to their guardians/parents and, at least in my case, they are our four-legged children.

Other women I know live far apart from their spouses, some of whom still identify as a couple. One woman lived in Hawaii and her husband lived on the west coast of the USA. They had regular visits with one another. She couldn't stand his family and he had work and family that he wouldn't leave the mainland for, but they 'still dug each other' and they made it work – a long-distance marriage where they both had their independent lives.

Another woman lived apart from her husband, in separate states and no longer a couple, but had a child, a history, and financial ties in common and just felt it wasn't worth the emotional and financial wrench to get a divorce. They were openly dating other people (of course keeping their private lives private from their child until it was time for a change in status).

Almost every woman I know nearby now does not share, or doesn't want to share a bedroom with their husbands. Some are unhappily married but staying together for a myriad of reasons. Some are happily married and identify as a couple.

I was fascinated to learn just how many women are creating these new (un) marriages and not letting dictates of religion, family tradition or society influence their actions anymore. These women recognize the need for personal space and the importance of sleep and restoration away from the demands of family and the world at large.

Some have husbands who snore but just find it easier and apparently preferable to give up the snuggle factor with another warm body in exchange for personal space. They wouldn't go back even if a cure for snoring was found!

While all women face burnout due to the continuing inequalities in the amount of work at home and outside the home, we always benefit mentally, emotionally, and physically from our own spaces, our sacred spaces. This is especially true for those of us who are highly sensitive, whether or not we have constant demands for attention from other people or situations.

As I started uncovering just how many women are in these 'alternative' marriages, what struck me is *how secret it is!* Only as I started getting to know women as good friends, or in the therapy room, did I find out how many people are in (un)marriages and just how many forms it takes. It seems true that 'sisters are doing it for themselves' as the famous song said.

It IS possible to have a marriage or an (un)marriage and not give up everything!

It IS possible to really take care of our own needs, have them recognized and respected and recharge ourselves with peace and quiet!

This shift needs to come out of the closet so it's time to 'be the change.' I have been collecting stories from women for an anthology so other women can know that there is a way to have a marriage or (un)marriage without the pain, longing and loss that so many women feel, whether they are in love with their spouses or not.

If both parties can have separate spaces and maturely negotiate what that all means for the relationship, everyone benefits, especially the children and pets. Perhaps we can truly appreciate the other person BETTER, whether a man or a same sex partner, lover or not, in a way we just can't when we live together. Once each person in a couple opens their mind to these possibilities, a road forward becomes more clear and less littered with the blame game.

I acknowledge that these kind of arrangements may be more possible to women with a certain amount of privilege who can have houses or apartments with multiple bedrooms or separate dwellings entirely. However, if more women knew about this, more of us could band together in co-housing to ease the financial burden, not live completely alone, yet not have to live completely together with a spouse or not-quite-ex-spouse. This is already happening.

"Every woman should have a boyfriend next door" may be the new modern take on Katherine Hepburn's quote.

My hope is to enlighten others about how many of us are choosing and crafting the new (un)marriages of the future. If you are interested in sharing your story for my upcoming book, please get in touch: jteleia@gmail.com

Collapse the Status Quo
Rev. Judith Laxer

Death throes are fierce. Stronger even than the ethos that keeps them alive. During death throes, the desperate grip tightens, greedy. A force of will more ferocious than any previous desire.

Oh Patriarchy, your futile attempt to turn back the clock, while the minutes drip out, a slow leak. Soon, the emptiness, the end.

But how soon?

We are safer steering clear, watching from a distance, but activists will tell you no. Do something. Facilitate and hasten this death. Wrench patriarchal rule from the clutch of fingers clutching money as power, yet soon to be nothing more than bones. Why wait?

The wrenchers and the planners.

What's the plan? Beyond ideology, what will replace this current outdated rule? What's our strategy, a blueprint even, a manual, something we can build from, the new design? Something with step-by-step instructions, and a timeline?

A coven convenes, Monday nights on the regular, to dissolve the insanity of patriarchal rule on the waning moon and build the matrifocal when it's waxing. They use the image and action of mycelium, the breaking down, the mushrooming, the eating, the consuming, the nourishing, the roots that reach everywhere, magic along the deep internal network, the expansion, and the vision. Between the worlds, the thread of the chant is taken up as paper is torn into shreds for the dismantling. Between the worlds, the thread of the chant shifts as fingers knit, tat, felt, or crochet, a sympathetic magic of creating the new (the ancient?) way, the sane way anyway. Sung into power, mycelium carries the magic where it knows it is needed. Expand dissolve expand dissolve expand dissolve again and again moon after moon power coursing underground underneath hidden invisible silent and strong as a virus.

After the death, will we have a funeral? Will we sing in exaltation? Will we cry with relief? Yes.

And when the ceremonies are over, when the song is through, when the tears have dried, then! Then we put women in every position of authority. Women. Only women. Women only. The other half, the better half, the kinder half, the ones who lead from their hearts not their pocket, the ones who do no harm, who refuse to send their children to kill other mother's children, who repudiate war, the ones who are not afraid to sit in council with one another, to listen and hear, to share their bounty and resources so everyone's needs are met, the ones who are willing to bury hatchets thrown by men ages ago, the patient ones who are willing to implement far sighted protocols with peace and love and healing at their core. Women, whose voices have been labeled emotional (as if that is a bad thing), silly, sentimental, foolish, ridiculous, and high maintenance, are now free to express. Women, who are not ashamed or humiliated to watch over the vulnerable, to care for those less fortunate, to remain present in a difficult situation. Women, who have cleaned up messes for so long they know how to prevent them. Women in power, fully empowered, wielding power, pure feminine power, intuitive power, in charge. At the helm of every household, every school, business, religion, and government. Women, the policy makers. Permission for everything must be sought from the women. Wise women. Old women. Bleeding women. Goddessmothers. Wisdom is the new order of the day. Women's wisdom holds sway.

Mycelium, reach within me too. Give death to the patriarch in me, and I shall not resist. Give rise to prudence in me, and compassion will lead. Expand and dissolve me too. Shoot your spores my way. I will take you in.

Birth Beyond Patriarchy
Evony Lynch

Time is running out. For the sake of our descendants, it is upon us now to recognise the runaway birthing train hurtling towards the apocalypse. A dystopian future where women simply no longer believe it is safe or even possible to birth their babies out of their vaginas. The age of industrialised birth is consuming us and soon our daughters and granddaughters will no longer remember a time when women birthed their babies in transcendent joy. We have embraced the mass marketed dogma that our inferior bodies require observation, manipulation and control to produce healthy offspring. We willingly submit to 'care' in centralised techno-units, give consent to extract our babies and accept the subsequent inescapable mental and physical trauma through deeply entrenched cognitive dissonance.

Industrialised birth is not new. We have a generation of midwives with no experience of undisturbed physiological birth and are now merely handmaidens of the national obstetric system. Year upon year we find new ways to disturb physiology and our innate capacity to grow and birth and feed a new human in the name of standardised safety.

In childhood I was called to this work, birthing my baby doll; creating a caesarean wound on another doll after the birth of my brother and watching any televised births I could find. My own birthing experience went from being strapped to a delivery bed crying out for pain relief with my first baby, to experiencing my inner power as I birthed my second 9lb 4oz baby at home. I know with all my being that I changed as a woman as I passed through that transformational birthing portal. Two years later I started my midwifery path. That is a birth truth. I want that for our future mothers.

Something is already stirring. Some women are making powerful autonomous choices, rejecting the conditioning of a patriarchal society that expects 'good mothers' to follow the rules of safe procreation. They are no longer compliant following protocols and subjecting themselves to the interventions of medical midwives. They are birthing freely. Alone and empowered.

Could this be the future; the antidote to the system that sets a new truth in motion?

Birth is inherently safe when left undisturbed but demands our respect. As a midwife of twenty years, I know there are golden nuggets of authentic midwifery wisdom that shouldn't be thrown out on a whim, that a wise woman in the corner knitting, with skills up her sleeve for a rare emergency is a useful human to have at a birth. Perhaps too, as I have been honoured to witness in the past year as a birthkeeper, some women don't want to be alone, they want to have a motherly wise figure to walk this journey with them.

Those women are already calling us. Since deregistering as a midwife, I now serve with my heart and hands, for the individual not the system. Legally I can no longer call myself a midwife, nor do I bring medical equipment to births, yet in being called to be present in this way, I see women rewriting what the medical establishment believe to be the truth about birth, because they have the freedom to follow their body, to labour and birth instinctively. I am finally witnessing everything I knew to be true.

My mantra has always been 'to keep birth truths alive'. My vision to achieve this is to create a community where we weave skills and knowledge, trust and respect; a haven for nurturing the wise women of the future, and a safe space for birthing. The time is calling us to step up, and not to be afraid. The witch wounding passed down through generations, and the persecution of midwives has led us to this place where we hold our tongue and are fearful of retribution. Yet birth is the cornerstone of life. Those of us who hold the knowledge of pregnancy and birth, through our work or our experience of growing and birthing babies are being called to birth this new way. We can take the science and the evidence of nurturing a healthy pregnancy and birth and weave it with the empirical wisdom of true midwives, birthkeepers and the birth stories of the mothers themselves. A middle way, cocreating a pathway to healthy and transformational childbearing.

The women are calling.
Our wombs are calling.
Our descendants are calling back through time.
I have been called.
Have you?

Embodied Education: Weaving our Way Beyond Mind. Radically rethinking learning and sharing spaces

Kay Louise and Dan Aldred

The question of who actually decides and directs what we 'should' learn is shady – and these decisions are frequently made by academics who are completely out of sync with students' interests. From our experience, there are government directives driven by an agenda of implanting into young people the narratives of patriarchy, capitalism, consumerism, and extraction.

Many current educational spaces are predominantly fear-based, hierarchical, head-only, and dissociative – places where unsafe relating occurs, as teachers often act out their own school trauma and patterning. We have noticed that the same issues that occur in traditional schooling environments can also arise in other spaces where people gather to learn and grow, such as personal development or spiritual arenas.

Bullying continues in spiritual communities, spaces, and practises. Patriarchal conditioning and school wounding is active in sharing circles. What was programmed in us at school – that we are never good enough, need to try harder, study more, achieve more – is being hijacked and monopolised by the wellness and personal growth industry, which tells us that we are broken and defective.

Sir Ken Robinson, an educator, author, and speaker, stated in his 2006 TED Talk, 'Do Schools Kill Creativity?' that "schools and our education system have mined our minds in the same way that we strip-mine the earth for a particular commodity. And for the future, it won't serve us. We have to rethink the fundamental principles on which we're educating our children."[*] This TED Talk has been viewed over 74 million times, so clearly it resonates with many.

In a recent survey, respondents described the current education system as 'competitive' (71.1%), 'goal-driven' (66%), 'controlled' (69.8%), 'demanding' (67.9%), 'critical' (64.2%) and driven by 'dominance' (64.2%). The YMCA charity website in 2016 featured an article on the 'negative educational experiences cause lasting damage to wellbeing'[†] which was based on the findings of their Eudaimonia research report.

Embodied Education is our vision for an educational paradigm based on wellbeing, coregulation and creativity. We advocate for body-first, relational and embodied approaches in organisations and communities.

We champion the creation of spaces which are trauma-informed and neurodivergent, sensory, and nervous system friendly. We support, celebrate, and encourage individuality, divergence, and innovation, alongside exploration, discovery, and imagination. We consider intuition (in addition to metacognition and critical thinking) to be a go-to point of reference and primarily, we believe gut instinct has the final say.

Edited and amended extract from *Embodied Education: Creating Safe Space for Learning, Facilitating and Sharing*, Kay Louise and Dan Aldred (2023).

---

[*] ted.com/talks/sir_ken_robinson_do_schools_kill_creativity
[†] ymca.co.uk/health-and-wellbeing/feature/negative-educational-experiences-cause-lasting-damagewellbeing

Grassroots

Sarah Featherstone

There is so much healing to be done. Globally, ancestrally, ecologically: healing from the wounds of patriarchy, imperialist and colonial iniquities – the list is long, and the legacy is profound. It affects all of us on so many levels, and it keeps on resurfacing in different forms. The healing work is ongoing, often being done by marginal groups who may not even consider it in this way.

Community arts, allotments, public libraries, and festivals, are just a few examples of spaces in which *the systemic prioritisation of private profit over human or social need bears a parasitic character.*‡

adrienne maree brown writes§ that if we are willing to undertake what she calls "the sacred work of practice", making life our practice ground and focusing energy where we have agency, we can exist as more than hungry ghosts in capitalism, we can begin to thrive. She encourages us to reclaim the sacred ground from which the world is made – our imaginations.

Part of my own work as a community artist and writer is facilitating creative wellbeing groups for people of all ages, many of whom are often struggling with anxiety and depression. It can be a struggle for some to make it to the groups, but when they do, the healing power of creative engagement usually works its magic. Making art in the company of others without judgement is energizing and connects people to the truth of their own visions and stories. It helps them transcend labels and diagnoses and the pressures, isolation and humiliating bureaucracy they have to face just to survive in capitalism.

As a single mum, I struggled to bring up my son in a system in which all the support structures of community have been stripped away. I quickly learnt that mothers who don't conform to the nuclear family norm are often judged and penalised financially. I was often lonely, isolated within the walls of my tiny flat, desperate for an accessible community space where I could go in the evenings for company and support, or a communal green space where my son could play

---

‡ Kennedy P (2017) *Vampire Capitalism: Fractured Societies and Alternative Futures.* London: Palgrave Macmillan

§ adriennemareebrown.net/2022/03/18/deep-practice

safely with other children. I'd seen this modelled when I volunteered at 'alternative' sustainable communities, but I didn't feel confident enough or able to make the leap into one by myself at that time. And once my son was enmeshed in the school system, it felt like another trapdoor had sprung shut.

It was the company of other single mothers, artists and outsiders who gave me strength and inspiration. I saw that there was a whole other way of living beneath the surface. Seeking out other ways of being has given me strength, resilience and compassion for myself and others who exist at the margins. We are like the 'weeds' who keep on coming back, rising up between the cracks no matter how much the perpetrators of toxic culture try to poison and repress us.

adrienne maree brown's concept of interconnectedness encourages us to draw on the strategies of other life-forms such as birds who migrate together each year for survival.* I am also reminded of the underground mycelial networks known as 'the Woodwide Web'† that offers us a model of radical interdependence: that we can take from the planet what we need to sustain ourselves as well as care for and protect it for ourselves and other more-than-human life forms. Some indigenous elders have indicated that we are entering a major transition time, and it's obvious that major change is approaching as the disruption to Earth's systems continues on a global scale. We can't rely on the so-called leaders to instigate a more sustainable and compassionate way of life. We have to join together at grass-roots level and make the journey ourselves.

---

* maree brown, adrienne (2017) *Emergent Strategy: Shaping Change, Changing Worlds*. AK Press
† science.org/content/article/wood-wide-web-underground-network-microbes-connects-trees-mapped-first-time

Woven Wild: Natural Embodiment

R. B. L. Robinson

The act of weaving is the ancient art of interlacing threads until they come together, forming a single piece of material crafted from entwined strands.

We too are woven. The threads of life are spun from the double-helix of DNA; we owe our existence to the information-rich braids of deoxyribonucleic acid that spiral within our cells. These chemicals at the core of our being are like interwoven yarns. Life is filled with twists and turns, and it is curious that the structure of our DNA reflects the winding path of life.

Life is often described as a tapestry, but we may not unpick the stitches. Past, present, and future are interwoven threads shaping life's pattern. But we can create a new design today. Each stitch counts, shaping the tapestry for future generations. Like warp and weft yarns, all life is interlaced. The existential angst many of us feel perhaps comes from the belief that life may unravel, and we may come apart at the seams.

When we are knit into being, we are wild, limitless potential. Once a fertilised egg begins the process of cell division, the first stitches of existence are sewn, and we understand a miracle: that life knows how to weave itself, in darkness. Yet from birth, the stitches that shape us become like ties that bind. We must unbind ourselves. We must go beyond concepts of power, hierarchy, and what is possible. There are no limitations apart from those set by the laws of nature. There is no hierarchy, only oneness.

Einstein suggested that gravity effects the fabric of space-time, causing it to curve. Science tells us energy and matter are one and the same, and energy never dies but simply changes form. We must embrace the curvaceous, intertwined nature of life and look beyond our definition of death. The matter and energy that is us will still exist, transformed, after we breathe our last.

Evolution takes time, but it is a process of growth. An essential part of our survival is to recognise our kinship with nature and to seek the threads of commonality, connection, and community between all that exists. For too long, nature has been viewed as separate to human beings; we are either outside of it, looking in longingly, or above, looking down greedily at how we can exploit what we perceive as beneath us and other. When we speak of feeling disconnected from our body, in the subtext of our words is hidden a severing, a sadness.

We yearn to be part of something bigger, to remember we are more than a mind in a body we have been taught to judge. We are part of nature. Our behaviour is led by a string of thoughts and beliefs, conditioned since birth. In seeking to live fully, we must remind ourselves of our corporeal nature, that we are blood and bone knit together to experience life.

So much of modern life sanitises the experience of the body. Our digital devices distract us from the reality of what it means to live, mind-full and body-full. We do not want to be with our thoughts for too long, or with the sensations of our body, so we numb ourselves, sever ourselves, first from ourselves and then from everything and everyone else, until we no longer see who we are.

We have lost our connection with our inner weaver. We no longer see the wilder pattern underpinning us. Instead, we see an unnatural pattern, where the stitches connecting mind and body, one being to another, and humanity to nature, have frayed.

This pattern works like an invisibility cloak – as soon as we put it on, it fits like a second skin, and we forget ourselves.

When we speak of our nature, we refer to our character, to what makes us different. Our individuality is important, and self-expression to be encouraged, but we ought to be wary of othering ourselves. We are in it together – you, me, and everyone else, and even that tree over there.

There is poetry in knowing we are ourselves and everything else, material and immaterial, a living breathing paradox, made of the same stuff as the universe – and there is a splendour in knowing, too, that someday, we will return as wildflower.

Embodiment is not simply about integrating our mind and body, but consciously remembering we are part of the body of the earth and cosmos.

The Ancient Greek word 'oikos', which gives us the word 'ecology', means 'home', 'family'. This planet is our home and everything that lives on it is our family. Wherever we are, we are home. We are equally as wild as the birds and trees.

We must no longer deny our true nature, or we risk never feeling at home anywhere. If we turn away from nature's beauty and muck, we turn away from ourselves, and from reality.

We are not separate from nature simply because we need to shelter from the elements to survive. Do we see a bird's nest as unnatural, separating the bird from its innate wildness, because it must weave a structure of twigs, moss, and grass around itself to survive?

We build walls around ourselves to protect ourselves from storms, but we do not need to build walls around our hearts.

We may create artificial divisions, but we do not have the power to shear the thread connecting us to all things; we only have the power to forget the thread exists.

We must look to the soil to see a better way. In root networks of trees, we find our own roots. In mycelium, those fungal threads of hyphae weaving through the earth, we find families of trees connecting, communicating, and caring for each other.

A woodland is a microcosm of life, woven in threads beneath our feet. We may struggle to see the wood for the trees, but nature holds the answers – an embroidery of existence, ever growing, ever changing, ever connected.

The Last Plane
Laetitia Devic

Lockdown
Our first experience of worldwide peace and quiet
We can hear the birds sing like never before
People who live near airports and train stations
Catch birdsong clearly and loudly for the first time –
Nearly as loud as a plane taking off or as a train departing

One day, lying down on my own on our trampoline
I see an aeroplane, high up in the blue sky
Forming a wispy trail behind it.
'What is this plane doing here?!'

In utter shock, I ask, 'What if this is the last plane?!'
Then words and questions keep coming…

What if planes stop flying from now on?!
This is the perfect opportunity!
No plane should resume flying now!
All but one airport per country shut down now!
Just ten planes fly every day
For medical emergencies and supplies only!

What we thought was impossible happened!
These past few weeks, all countries agreed
In one swoop, to shut down all airports,
To stop flying in the name of our survival
Can't we do the same in the name of the Earth's survival?

I am now incensed and passionate
This is what we need to do!
This is what the Earth needs from us!
This is what our precious planet is demanding of us!

What started as an innocent, playful question
Now has become a very serious one.

I am met with silence.
I am too far ahead.
I am always too far ahead of the pack
With my ideas and visions.

I didn't say much publicly for three years,
Then I started telling people and the world
That I was avoiding flying, for the planet and for our children
That I was taking the train but not the plane.

Sure, that's a privilege.
Is it, though?

Yes, for the planet, we MUST sacrifice ourselves

Yes, for the planet, we may have to sacrifice our dreams
Yes, these changes for the planet's health
Require awareness, consciousness and a paradigm shift

Saving the planet starts with us
And what we're required to sacrifice to get there.

Edited version of The Last Plane *by Laetitia Devic.*

One Day
Suzanne Dance

One day
Children will ask their teachers
What was war?
It is up to us
To bring that day to be
Maybe it is this day.

Extract from One Day, *Suzanne Dance.*

PRAYERS, PRACTICES AND RITUALS

White Spirit & Silver Hands

Julie Erwin

May We Reclaim

Vanya Leilani PhD

In order to live in obedience to patriarchal ideologies, we must live with a denigrated female, an elevated male at war with the land, disconnected from the sacredness of the Earth and body, and severed from the ways of being and knowing associated with the images of the feminine sacred. We must turn on our ourselves and our inner knowing. As we question the status quo and trust our dis-ease with these bargains, these curses become more visible. As we transgress through seeing them, naming them, and challenging them, it often feels as if they are tightening and intensifying.

May we reclaim a vision of a humanity that knows in its bones, in its soft rolling flesh, and in its warm pulsating bloodlines that it belongs to a much greater ecological system that includes the more-than-human world, that is part of One Flesh, that belongs to the world of animals, trees, soil, and rain.

May we reclaim what has been largely lost in Western modernity, that is, a human sense of deep connection, of mutual participation, and of unwavering belonging with and to Nature. In this vision, we return to what we are made of, or more accurately, we *see* what we are made of and feel it with our fingertips, catch its scent, taste its depths. We feel Nature's cadence beating in the depths of our bodies.

May we unravel the curse of disenchantment and return to wild belonging and old knowing. May we return to our roots and learn to participate in the great web of life of which we are a part of and enter consciously into the wild dance of the universe.

This is re-enchantment.

May this curse be banished over and over again as we choose to follow our knowing beyond the boundaries of our indoctrination to be good. When all we can see is ruin and all we can feel is desolation, may the seeds buried in our lives begin to glow with warmth and promise. When it seems like there is only one story and one way, may we hear the distant echoes of our ancestors and allies reminding us that there are many stories and many ways. From the interwoven intricacy of a spider web to the complexity of how galaxies reach for one another, may we witness and be reminded of the beautiful multiplicity and interconnection of Nature and that, truly, we can never fall out of what we are made of. We are made of earth and stardust; our belonging is deep and expansive and irrevocable."

Extract from *The Flesh and the Fruit: Remembering Eve and the Power of Creative Transgression*, Vanya Leilani PhD, Womancraft Publishing (2024).

A Birthing Journey
Kelly Barrett

What began as an imaginary romp through the land of the Great Magic, the landscape inhabited by the Wild Woman, became a grounded form of story activism in my research project, Rewilding the Feminine. A temporal village was created for change agents to explore how to embody and cultivate the instinctual nature of the feminine, co-creating an alternative narrative to the culture of patriarchy. Yet, for any rewilding effort to be successful and sustainable, reintroduction must occur in a supportive and hospitable environment.

By restoring our Wild Woman, we were enacting a version of the heroine's journey. The gift we brought back was our more intact self. The village we were returning to, however, was toxic.

Many of us in our culture have embarked on a heroine's journey. Collectively, as we return, we coalesce as a larger and larger presence. Miraculously and magically we have alchemized ourselves while in the poisonous amniotic waters in the womb of patriarchy.

Pregnancy is a watery affair. Some of us have been on the journey, gestating in the underworld a long time. It has been languid and dreamy, following the mystery of symbolic guidance and synchronicities into the depths. There is, though, a danger of staying too long, getting caught in an endless loop of seeking perfection. And perfection is a patriarchal construct that keeps us submerged. While our magic is alluring on the heroine's journey, it does not end there. In fact, it may not be until our return when we find each other, joining together, that we discover our full capacity and exert our most potent effect in the world. We do not have to remain in the pregnant belly, the patriarchal village of our conception. We can journey down the birth canal, and be born into new virgin territory. The contractions may be violent and painful, but we are being called to go beyond the heroine's journey. We are being beckoned into an even larger and wider and broader landscape, to become a partner in a lived story of wholeness.

In this liminal world, we arrive provisioned with what we have learned. We are viable creatures for a partnering culture. We are the healing elixir, here to break the cultural trance tilted towards destruction and bereft of creation and beauty. We blaze a new trail in a territory of our own collective making, in a land beyond Patriland, and it can only be reached if we are willing to cut the umbilical cord.

Wielding our wands of creativity, wild women grown into wise women, we crystallize what we have imagined, enact it, build it, and embody it. Our new myth, our new lived story, spreads like an algal bloom as a new technicolor vision emerges.

Where the heroine's journey is a healing journey, this is a birthing journey.

We Do Not Consent: A Prayer of Resistance Magic

Sarah Robinson

Light a candle and take a deep breath; sisters and soulkin. We will gather our strength and unite in purpose. Let us say it together, as one.

WE DO NOT CONSENT

We do not consent to a world plagued by sexism, misogyny, racism, capitalism, and the destruction of our planet.

We reject the rules of patriarchy and the systems that perpetuate inequality and division. We stand together and declare our dissent.

With our rallying cry, we summon our power, creating a beacon of hope.

We may take action in ways that are right for us, however small or large they may be.

We will advocate for change and work to dismantle these oppressive structures.

If ever there was a time for us to come together, stand together, rebel together, it is now.

We can embrace our shared experiences as all who connect to what it is to be woman and connect to the feminine. We are different, but we are sisters.

Blow out the candle; we will not be bound by patriarchy. Let us be the light that illuminates the path to a new world, and walk forward towards it. A world where justice, equality, and love are sovereign.

Let us unite, let us be heard. Together. Together, we will be the light.

Plant Medicine Poetry: Thistle
Melissa Rose Spencer

Thistle
Thank you for your medicine
I accept your teachings
I reclaim my feminine
Fierce protection and boundaries
Banish those who are unbidden
Fierceness is not weakness
To be gentle requires strength
A warning to passers by
Who approach with prowess
Here I stand
Heed these spines my feet deep in the land
Stronger than before.

Extract from *Thistle*, Melissa Rose Spencer.

A Spell for Uncertain Times
Lise Lønsmann

I unbelong myself to a world of control, of winning, of buying and selling bombs, of planning the next attack, of unhealed father wounds wreaking havoc, of inner conflict and chaos playing out in the outer world.

I let myself grieve the old, while I hum a soft prayer to a peaceful, wise goddess.

I belong myself to unlearning the old ways. To untangling and dismantling.

I belong myself to a new world, to new ways of being and co-existing. Ways that are deeply rooted in shared intentions and core values of co-creation, sustainability and respect for life and that hold space for differences and disagreements, in wise and peaceful ways.

I belong myself to the inspiration that is brewing in my belly and to the excitement in my hands and fingertips, for the new world that I want to be a part of and contribute to.

I belong myself to creativity and magic, to learning and exploring, to connecting and deepening.

To a vision that breathes life into me.

To building and rebuilding together.

To meaningful community.

I belong myself to humility and gratitude.

And I belong myself to belonging. Because that brings my heart peace.

Earth, Sky and Breath: A Grounding Exercise
Helen Smith

Current times are rocky, and the transition to a post-patriarchal society won't be smooth all the way. If we're going to get through it happy and healthy, we're going to need some tools to centre and ground ourselves. Tools that help us reconnect to ourselves, and to the natural world. I would like to offer a short exercise which I find very beneficial, developed from my practice as a druid and hypnotherapist.

This exercise can be done in just a couple of minutes, wherever and whenever you need a moment to ground and reconnect. You may also like to practice outdoors, with bare feet on the earth or your face tipped to the sun, or simply pull a chair up to an open window, for a deeper connection to nature. Please adapt this exercise to your own situation, needs and body. Listen to your body, and only do what feels good. It is my sincere hope that you will find something here that brings you joy, tranquillity, connection, and stability.

- Close your eyes if this is comfortable for you, and notice your breath. How low in your body can you sense the movement of breath? See if you can place your awareness here for a moment. Your breathing may slow and deepen, but there is no need to try and control the breath. Let it come and go as it wishes. Allow yourself to be breathed. Supported effortlessly by the breath.

- Gently become aware of the earth below you. Feel the contact between your feet and the earth. Notice how it holds you, cradles you, supports you. Take a moment in this awareness. Then, take a deep breath with the earth: in through the nose, hold for a moment, and out through the mouth. Breathe the energy of the earth.

- Become aware of the sky above you. Feel its vastness, and the temperature and sensation of the air on your skin. The atmosphere wraps the earth in an embrace, protecting it, and us, and creating the conditions necessary for life. Take a moment with this awareness. Then, take a deep breath with the sky: in through the nose, hold for a moment, and out through the mouth. Breathe the energy of the sky.

- Feel yourself centred between earth and sky, nourished and nurtured by them both. Take a moment in this awareness. Then, take a deep breath with yourself. Sense your own energy, strong and healing, within you.

- Continue to rest in this space, feeling held by earth, sky and breath, for as long as you choose.

- When you are ready to close, place your hands on your heart, thanking yourself for taking these moments to reconnect and replenish. Gently open your eyes, and offer yourself a smile.

- Offer the earth and sky a thank you, or send them a blessing, to close.

She Will Not Fight

AnnaMarie Laforest White

She will open the windows
to blow out the dust,
she will bring in the flowers
– so many stems –
and put the ladder against the tree
for bringing in the fruit.
She will let the neighbors in,
their butterflies and bugs
welcome at her hearth.
She will show the children
how to paint with light
and urge them take it home.
She will remind the babies
what they have to do.
She will not fight,
but she will change everything.
She will put on her boots
and glasses
and visit all the countries.
She will soothe the ravaged
with bulbs and seeds from her pockets
quilts from her pack,
landscapes changing
as light from her eyes
filters to the ground
new pools forming
as the indents of her giant boots
fill with rain.

She will come home
wash her hands at her sink

and put on her biggest hat
  to go with us on our quests.
  She is so tall
  the flowers on her brim
  illuminate our steps
  and she will be there
  to catch those who collapse.
  She will not fight.
  She will change everything.

A Ritual for Letting Go of the Patriarchy

Charlotte Louise Wylde

This is a ritual for letting go of the hold that patriarchy has over us, even if we are not aware of the ways in which it has affected our lives. It will take approximately thirty minutes, but can take longer if you would like it to. Try to find a quiet space either indoors or outside where interruptions can be minimised. It is designed to be practiced alone but can be adapted for more people if you have a group. You will need:

- Salted water
- Incense or room spray
- Compass (may not be necessary)
- A scarf
- Writing / drawing materials
- A means of playing music

The ritual

Set up your ritual space by first cleansing the area – this can be done by sprinkling salted water clockwise in a circle around you, or visualising white light in the room, or with reiki symbols at each corner.

Consecrate the area by wafting incense smoke in a circular space around you or spraying at each corner with room spray.

Draw a circle around you with your finger or a wand. This creates a safe working space for your magick. It keeps the ritual energy focused and prevents distractions from the ordinary world creeping in.

Face each cardinal direction, beginning with East and working round in a clockwise direction. Say some welcoming words to each direction as you go, such as: 'spirit of the East, hail and welcome.'

Your space is now elementally balanced.

Ask the Goddess to join you and state your wish for her aid in releasing your attachment to the patriarchy.

Tie the scarf around your mouth to symbolise being silenced. If this is too triggering for you, imagine it being there.

Spend some time quietly meditating upon the feelings that arise whilst the scarf is restricting your verbal expression. You may also wish to close your eyes whilst you contemplate.

Consider the ways in which living within a patriarchal system has affected you; have you been able to feel, to express, to act, to rest freely? You could write down your thoughts and feelings or draw pictures.

When you are ready, ask in your mind for the aid of the Goddess to release you from the restrictions of the patriarchy. Feel her hands untying the scarf for you – untie it as you do.

When your mouth is finally free, say something out loud, anything. Whatever it is it will be perfect for the time and place.

Once you have uttered the words that come to you, play some upbeat music that you enjoy. Take a minute or so to move with abandon and sing to the track. Revel in the feelings of release and freedom that the Goddess has given to you.

When you are ready to close the ritual, thank the Goddess and any unseen helpers. Thank the elements starting North and turning anticlockwise to each direction in turn.

Unwind your circle in an anticlockwise direction using your finger or a wand; allowing the energies you have raised to integrate with the ordinary world.

Energetically cleanse your space using whichever method you used at the beginning for example sprinkling salted water.

Remember to ground well after a ritual – especially before you have to do anything such as driving. You can do this by eating something, having a hot drink, going for a walk or holding a rock.

Over the next two weeks, when you remember the ritual, say out loud, the words 'I am now free.'

We Will Not Be Lost To These Times
Eleanor Brown

I've been living in the wasteland I've been clinging in the dark
I've been hearing all these voices and losing hope and heart
From a lineage of silence now I break the biggest vow
So I'm rising from these ashes and speaking truth to power

So come back from these edges in this wilderness of mind
On a bruised and broken planet that renews without our kind
This is more than just my story this is written in the land
In the roots amongst the fir trees, yes, we rise to overcome

We will not be lost to these tides
No we will not be lost to these tides
We will not be lost to these times
No we will not be lost to these times.

Extract from the song 'We Will Not Be Lost to These Times', Eleanor Brown.

Tending to Hope in Embodied Ways
Lise Lønsmann

When the deadness of patriarchy overwhelms me
I pause and breathe
I slow down and create space

I hum a soft lullaby to soothe the parts of me that feel lost
I place a hand on my heart to feel its steady rhythm, and I let it ground me
I invite the wisest, softest parts within me to step forward, into an inner council
I share gratitude
I practice deep listening, so I can hear the wisdom they are whispering to me
I remember myself back to who I truly am
That is what I do, when the deadness of patriarchy overwhelms me
When systems of control make me feel powerless
When fear starts to take root in my heart
When I am exhausted from disconnecting from myself

I pause and breathe
I place a hand on my heart to feel its steady rhythm, and I let it ground me

I unbelong myself to the deadness
And remind myself
That the most sacred part of me and all humans
Is our sacred aliveness
The life energy that moves through us all
The creativity we all possess
The deeply inspired parts of us that want to contribute and co-create and be a part of something
The playfulness that makes our body quiver with excitement and expectation

The parts of us that make us feel most alive
The parts of us that we have been taught to forget

I remember those parts, when patriarchy overwhelms me
I pause and breathe
I place a hand on my heart to feel its steady rhythm, and I let it ground me

I close my eyes and tune into a grounded place within myself
Sometimes this makes me sad because I remember the decades of feeling lost
Because I had no idea that that grounded place existed
But nowadays I know that grounded place so well

I have cultivated a close relationship with it
   And I keep coming back to it, again and again
   When the ground underneath me is shaken
   When I feel like the chaos of the world is going to swallow me up
   When I forget to listen to my inner guidance

I pause and breathe
I place a hand on my heart to feel its steady rhythm, and I let it ground me

There is a deep knowing here that feels familiar and unfamiliar at the same time
This grounded place within me reminds me of the vastness of my inner landscapes
I can see far, and at the same time I know
That there are unknown places within me too
Places that I have avoided
Places that I have been taught to fear
Places that I have been taught to forget

So I pause and breathe
And drop deeper into my body, deeper into presence
I feel my feet against the floor
And my lungs expand and contract with every breath

With my eyes closed and my hand on my heart I remind myself
That there is hope here
In this grounded place
I sit with hope
I know that it is my responsibility to keep it alive
To shield it, to stay with it, to return to it often
To keep coming back to it and tend to it, so it does not die

I make this an embodied practice
I feel into my grounded place and my hope that lives here
With all parts of me

I notice where hope is alive in my body
I cultivate a deep relationship with hope

Because I know that tending to my hope in embodied ways
Is the doorway to my sacred aliveness
An aliveness that drives me
And keeps me awake and connected
While navigating a culture of disconnect

That is what I do, when the deadness of patriarchy overwhelms me
I pause and breathe
I place a hand on my heart to feel its steady rhythm, and I let it ground me
I carefully tend to my hope that lives in the grounded place within me
And I remember myself back to sacred aliveness

Know

Léa-Jeanne Sachot

They will burn your tents
but they can't burn the moon
and the moon will call your blood
so you may remember
and your blood will be blessed
again
you will weave the world with your womb
again
and you will create the world
to the image of your dreams
and your dreams will guide you home
into old lands of wisdom
you were born to
share

Burning Woman
Lucy H. Pearce

These are burning times. And they call for Burning Women. Women embodying their passion. Women feeling in their bodies. Creative women. Courageous women. Connected women.

Gather the women. Gather the men. Gather all the Burning Ones. Let us come together in ecstatic creative partnership. In dangerous acts of creative rebellion.

Rip your clothes off, run towards the flames and dance like there's no tomorrow to the beat of your own heart. Only you can hear the rhythm, only you know its tune, only your body can dance this way, so do it. Stop holding back, and waiting, and trying to do it right, and not upset anyone.

I am there right beside you. I see your courage, I sense your power, I hear your voice. You are not alone.

We are ready. We hold the torches, we circle. We are the carriers of life-giving flames. We burn from the inside. The Feminine inflammation, a conflagration of sisters, burning away the bitter past and lighting the way to the future.

It is time.
Will you join us?
We often fear that the Revolution needed is too big for what we can give.
Too much change is required inside, outside.
And we are too small.
But all that is required is that you step into the truth of your life.
And speak it, write it, paint it, dance it.
That you shine your light on your truth, for the world to see.
And as hundreds, then thousands, then millions do this – each sparking the courage of yet more –
Suddenly we have a world alight with truth.
We are shifting ourselves.
We are shifting the world.
Dancing her into a new orbit.

We are filling in the space where our voices were silenced

Filling in the blanks where our images have been lacking.

We are weaving her-story into reality.

Unweaving the limiting his-stories.

Creating our-story.

Reaching beyond religion and patriarchy and capitalism and so-called democracy.

Into new ways of being and seeing.

We are the bridge between worlds

We are the ones we have been waiting for.

Arise, Burning Woman!

Arise, Burning Women!

Extract from *Burning Woman*, Lucy H. Pearce, Womancraft Publishing (2016).

Contributors

Adele Mower (p. 61) is a disabled writer who dwells in the heartbeat of Hull, one of the UK's most deprived cities. She has a deep love of the land, both urban and rural, and is honoured to follow in the footsteps of the many strong Hull women who paved the way. Instagram: @adele.m.mower

Agnieszka Drabek-Prime (p. 93) is a teacher, Womb Medicine Woman, and Sacred Weaver. Through connection with the Spirit, from threads of different traditions as well as from the wisdom of her womb and the Sacred Feminine, she is weaving sacred into everyday life. She lives in Cambridge, UK, teaching, seeing clients, organizing ceremonies and courses in person and on-line. primetherapy.co.uk · Instagram: @yoni.wise

Alison Newvine (p. 104) is a psychotherapist, spiritual consultant and musician living in northern California. Her writing is featured in publications by Mago Academy and Girl God Books. With her band, Spiral Muse, she writes and produces music dedicated to the Goddess and sacred feminist visions. alisonnewvine.org · Facebook: @spiralmuseband.

Amy Wilding (pp. 70, 96) is a queer and inclusive feminist, author, and international speaker. With a passion for empowering women by helping them to reclaim their inherent sovereignty and wisdom, she has been leading sacred women's circles, mother-daughter circles, and rite-of-passage ceremonies for well over a decade. She is the author of *Wild & Wise: Sacred Feminine Meditations for Women's Circles & Personal Awakening*. She is also a National Board Certified Integrative Women's Health Coach, and offers one-on-one and small group coaching focusing on menstrual cycle literacy, including menarche and perimenopause. redtentlouisville.com · Instagram: @redtentlouisville

AnnaMarie Laforest White (p. 154) is a poet, holistic health instructor, music lover and flower photographer who lives near a beautiful river in Maryland, USA. Her writing has appeared in Washington DC, Texas, Australia, and even on a cereal box in Oregon.
annamarielaforest.wixsite.com/stories · Instagram: @amlstories

Anne Reeder Heck (p. 75) is a writer, healer, artist and fierce believer in miracles. Author of *A Fierce Belief in Miracles*, and *Float on Leaves*, Anne is devoted to guiding others to trust themselves, open to their intuition, and experience life's magic. She lives in Asheville, North Carolina. anneheck.com · @anneheck1

Beverley Pannell (p. 113) lives in Sussex with her partner and young daughter. She runs Motherhood Uncensored, a charity tackling the myths, misogyny and nonsense surrounding modern motherhood. Beverley likes to spend weekends café-hopping but increasingly spends them stopping her toddler falling off slides.
motherhood-uncensored.org · Instagram: @uncensored_motherhood_stories

Carly Mountain (p. 106) is a somatic psychotherapist and the author of *Descent & Rising: Women's Stories & the Embodiment of the Inanna Myth*, published by Womancraft Publishing. She is passionate about facilitating women to remember and reconnect with their inherent erotic aliveness, power and pleasure. She lives in Sheffield, England with her husband and two daughters.
carlymountain.com · Instagram: @carly_mountain

Carol Watts (p. 14) is an emerging writer primarily in the genre of Creative fiction Nature/Memoir. She lives in the Pacific Northwest on Vancouver Island, Canada, within a few minutes' walking distance of breathtaking forest and ocean trails that inspire her writing.

Caryl Church-Jesseph M.A., (she/her) (p. 77) is an award winning art educator, artist and writer in Ohio, Great Lakes Region of North America. She is creator of Phia Creative Arts which offers arts and nature-based programming. Caryl is currently writing a book about the meaningful relationships people have with trees.

Contributors

Caryn MacGrandle (p. 96) is the creator of the Divine Feminine App: an online community since 2016 that has been connecting women (all genders) in Circles, events and resources. She has participated in numerous online and location events such as the World Parliament of Religions.
theDivineFeminineApp.com

Dr. CL Nash (p. 85) is a Research Fellow at the University of Edinburgh's School of Social and Political Science and current recipient of the Writing Fellowship with the Johannesburg Institute for Advanced Studies (JIAS). Dr. Nash's forthcoming book with SCM Press (2025) provides an entrée to womanist theology in the UK. She directs the Misogynoir to Mishpat Research Network, which moves from "hatred of Black women to justice" by amplifying African-descended women's academic contributions through mentoring, resource sharing, and seminars.
misogynoir2mishpat.wordpress.com · misogynoir2mishpat.substack.com

Charlotte Louise Wylde (p. 155) lives and works in Leicester, UK. She is a bellydancing former psychiatrist who blends witchcraft, shamanism and tarot with conventional counselling techniques to help rekindle the inner flame. She loves to dance and to swim outdoors.
goddesscounselling.com · Instagram: @goddess.counselling

Coco Oya Cienna-Rey (p. 12) is a UK-based creative, mystic, soul guide and writer. Author of Digging for Mother's Bones, published by Womancraft Publishing. Her creativity is informed by her journey as a devotee of the Tantric path (an embodied path of self-liberation) and being a channel for the Divine Feminine. Deeply sensitive and highly empathic she can be found weaving her intuitive gives at creativelycoco.com

Donna Donnabella (p. 92) is a retired educator and creative soul who lives in central New York state gardening, communing with nature, writing, and finding the infinite in the everyday through her creative endeavors.
GardensEyeView.com · Instagram: @ddonabella

D'Vorah J. Grenn En-Kohenet, Ph.D (p. 66) educator, priestess, ordained Mashpi'ah/spiritual guide and lineage-holder of a female Kabbalist tradition, founded The Lilith Institute. She co-directed the Women's Spirituality MA Program, ITP/Sofia University, and was a founding theorist of the Kohenet movement. Author of *Lilith's Fire: Talking to Goddess*, sacred writings from seventy-two women in twenty-five traditions. She lives in California. lilithinstitute.com · Instagram: @lilith_institute

Edel Murphy (p. 58) lives in Lismore, Ireland. She loves to write short stories and poetry. Her career is a privilege and involves working with teenagers and young adults. She self-published a book called *For Myself During Hard Times*, dealing with themes of loss and love.

Eleanor Brown (p. 157) is a songwriter and music-maker who connects deeply with the natural world and the changing times, creating from both the descent and the rising. She lives in the UK. eleanorbrown.bandcamp.com

Elen Jones (p. 28) is a poet, painter and performance artist living in Canterbury. She is the author of an oracle deck 'The Voices of the Dark Mothers.' Her passions are nerding, magic, and social justice. Facebook / Instagram: @spiralpriestess

Elisabeth "Paisley" Preitauer (p. 80) writes daily in her little green chair in Eugene, Oregon, US. Having spent 30+ years working fulltime in big cities, the peacefulness will always soothe. She has four industrious adult children and two cutie grands who love to visit because "Grammy and Grampy are silly". The long journey from conventional to counter culture was rough and full of surprises. Paisley likes to dance, make strangers laugh and just sit enjoying her thoughts.

Enna Rose Andrews (p. 89) lives on the Hove seafront, England. She LOVES being held between the ocean and South Downs. Her work revolves around embodiment. She is a Massage Therapist and a Care Worker for human and non human animals. She has no online presence and can be contacted at Ennaandrews@gmail.com

Eve Smith (p. 19) Working with transformative practices to develop sovereignty of the Self, Eve Smith is passionate about using story and Sound as medicine. Eve tailors her weekly newsletter to the I Ching and energetic practices. She works as a Sound and Reiki practitioner in Atlanta, GA, US.
evesmyth.substack.com

Evony Lynch (p. 135) is a deregistered midwife, with over twenty years' experience in attending births, specialising in supporting homebirth and births outside of guidelines. She practices as a birthkeeper, writer and podcaster based in Cornwall. Her mantra has always been 'to keep birth truths alive' and now teaches aspiring birthkeepers.

Georg Cook (p. 40) is a poet, writer, over-thinker and nature spiritualist living on the Sussex Coast of the U.K. She is on a powerful journey of self-rediscovery following Narcissist Abuse through the healing power of nature, especially the Sea and the seasons. She is a current contributor to the Earth Pathways 2024 wall calendar.
earthpathwaysshowcase.uk/contributors/cook_georg.html · @georgcook_writer

Ger Moane (p. 84) is a psychologist, writer and shamanic practitioner. She was born in Galway and currently lives in Dublin. She has been a full-time writer of fiction for several years. She has written a novel and short stories about ancient Ireland, and also writes about LGBTQ+ issues. germoane@gmail.com

Gillian White (p. 63) is a seasoned facilitator of women's circles, public speaker, metaphysical teacher, and soul worker, and she resides in Alberta's scenic Foothills, Canada. With expertise across many spiritual disciplines, she delves into clients' inner worlds, uncovering the roots of challenges, guiding profound soul connections, and nurturing transformative spiritual practices.
gillian-white.com · @weaving_soul_magick

Hazel Evans (pp. 29, 53) is an award-winning visionary artist, with the gift of foresight, Hazel is a medicine woman with a powerful journey of reclaiming her heart through the shamanic life of living art and animism. An inspirational leader and mentor of deep feminine wisdom, mysteries of creation and author of the Soul Prophecy Oracle.
thesovereignjourney.com · Instagram: @thesovereignjourney

Helen Smith (pp. 129, 152) is a neurodivergent creative from the Welsh Marches, currently residing in a castle in Fife, Scotland. With a background in zoology and psychology, she can often be found wandering the woods, knitting small cats, or painting mythic feminine archetypes.
helensmithwrites.com · @earth.body.art

Jane Catherine Severn (p. 126) psychotherapist, Femenome® therapist, educator and writer, lives in Aotearoa (New Zealand). Jane is the founder and facilitator of Luna House and author of *The World Within Women: the femenome guide to your menstrual cycle*. Her second book, on menopause, is expected later in 2024.
lunahouse.co.nz · Facebook: @lunahousewomen

Jeanne Teleia (p. 131) LMFT, Play Therapist, Holistic Life, Wellness and Family Coach lives in France and teaches people how to be resilient and live in alignment with their true essence. Being a 'Fun Finder', she uses the power of nature and peak experiences to help people (re)gain their birthright – JOY. She is currently writing a book on menopause, and invites your stories and experiences around changing the conversations around it. Email jteleia@gmail.com to be part of this change! YourLifeWellLived.net

Jennifer Eva Pillau (p. 119) a mother of two, holds a bachelor's degree in business administration, a master's degree in Traditional Chinese Medicine, and a certification in Ayurvedic Practice. She studies matriarchal societies and matriarchal theory at International Academy Hagia, Germany. She is an experienced facilitator of Red Tent circles for women and currently lives on the Island of Crete. Her pen name is the name of her mother's Estonian lineage.
heartwombandsoul.com

Contributors

Jennifer Miller (p. 18) is from the North Georgia mountains and currently resides in Alabama, US. She explores themes of earth-centered spirituality and women's empowerment in her poems and prose. Her works have appeared in *Rebelle Society, SageWoman*, and several feminist anthologies.
quillofthegoddess.com · Instagram / Facebook: @quillofthegoddess

Rev. Jo Royle (p. 21) is an Interfaith Minister and Creatrix of ceremony. She's passionate about healing the patriarchal wounds of the feminine and our beautiful earth. She LOVES to craft meaningful and magical ceremonies, for herself and others, especially nature based, in the wilds of the Isle of Skye, her home.
revjoroyle.co.uk · @revjoroyle

Rev. Judith Laxer (p. 133) is a modern-day mystic who believes that humor, beauty, and the wonders of nature make life worth living. The founding Priestess of Gaia's Temple and author of Along the Wheel of Time: Sacred Stories for Nature Lovers, Judith dedicates her work to the Divine Feminine.
gaiastemple.org · Facebook: @Gaia's Temple Seattle

Julie Armstrong (p. 51) lives in Cheshire. She is a Nature writer, folklorist and yogini. Walking the land is central to her creative practice. She has a PhD in Creative Writing, publications include: *The Magic of Wild Things, A Wild Calling, Walking the Celtic Wheel, The Root & the Wing*.
Facebook: @Julie.armstrong.3323

Julie Erwin (p. 147) at the beginning of her seventh decade, lives on the Pennines in East Lancashire, a place of wild moors and narrow valleys. She is stepping into art and writing, reclaiming things lost way back when and living her autistic, authentic self. Insideoutsideautism.blog · Instagram: @jaeerwin63

Juno (p. 92) is a 12-year-old who enjoys creative writing and singing. She is currently home-schooled and learning interesting things like British Sign Language and horse riding. She lives in Bristol, UK, with her family and two cats.

Kate Ward (p. 18) lives in Ogden, Utah, US. She's a fiber artist that specializes in woven tapestries inspired by nature and the land around her. She also creates workshops for other creatives and artists based around the seasons and cycles within and around us. Instagram @thewovenriver

Katia Wallace (p. 41) is a home educator, teacher and eco-feminist. She was born in France and has lived in Australia, the United States, Austria and Scotland. She currently lives in England with her family. She home educates her children and works in a French community school. In her free time she enjoys gardening, cooking, writing, reading, and the creative arts. theearthkeepersway.com · Instagram: @theearthkeepersway

Kay Louise Aldred (p. 137) lives in rural North Yorkshire and is an experienced and nervous system informed teacher, researcher, and published author of four books. Kay specialises in spiritual needs, care and wellbeing, embodied ways of knowing and neurodiversity. She is an Associate at Neurodiverse Connection. kaylouisealdred.com · Instagram / X / LinkedIn: @kaylouisealdred

Kelle BanDea (p. 16) is a neurodivergent mother of three with Traveller heritage. She currently lives in Warwickshire in the UK with her partner, children and a varied assortment of animals. Her first two books, *Modron: Meeting the Celtic Mother Goddess* and *Mabon: Discovering the Celtic God of Hunt and Harp* are forthcoming from Moon Books.

Kelly Barrett (pp. 33, 149) is a researcher, writer, artist, and yogini, living in the Sangre de Cristo Mountains of New Mexico and on the northern coast of California. She completed a research study *The Great Magic, Rewilding the Feminine* in 2018 as part of her MA in Consciousness and Transformative Studies. You can contact her at kelly@madzoga.com · 101eyes.com

Kimberly Moore (p. 35) is a Priestess and Daughter of Goddess. She is the Founder of MotherHouse of the Goddess and Mystery School of the Goddess. Kimberly lives in Delaware with her kitty and more than 250 images of deity. Her days are filled with mantra, teaching, writing, and lots of Goddesses. motherhouseofthegoddess.com

Laetitia Devic (p. 143) is a Book, Business and Life Doula. Owner of Nesting Mums, she supports women with writing, business and motherhood. She helps mums and their families to overcome trauma, anxiety, stress, overwhelm and writing blocks. nestingmums.uk · Instagram: @nestingmums

Léa-Jeanne Sachot (p. 160) is an Embodied Mindfulness facilitator, Menstrual Cycle Wisdom mentor, Womb-Healing artist, and Earth activist. She currently lives in France and Spain and offers 1:1 mentoring and healing sessions, workshops, and women's circles online. Her womb-poetry was born from a flow-writing, singing; blood-painting experience during her moon-time meditation. You can contact her at ljsachot@gmail.com

Linda Sewallius Katz (p. 25) is a writer, women's life coach, dream whisperer and Qoya Inspired Movement teacher. She is the author of *Homecoming: One Woman's Story of Dismantling the Inner Cage* and *Freeing Her Wild Feminine Soul*. She resides in Plano, Texas, US with her beloved husband Eric and puppy Ursa. singingbirdcoaching.com · Instagram: @singingbirdcoaching

Lise Lønsmann (pp. 152, 157) is a trauma-informed somatic practitioner, an embodiment mentor and a circle facilitator. She supports heart-led women in connecting deeper with their body and its wisdom to heal old inner wounds and create safety in the body and inner world. Lise lives in Vejle, Denmark. liseloensmann.com · Instagram: @liseloensmannhealing

Liset Dettingmeijer (p. 11) lives in the Netherlands and is a nature-loving creatrix, focusing on personal growth. The last few years she has been exploring (in words and images) feminine archetypes. The Witch is one of many who has a special place in her heart and life. liset-dettingmeijer.nl

Looby MacNamara (pp. 27, 122) is an author, teacher, designer, artist and mother. She is co-creator of the Cultural Emergence toolkit. She is one of the partners of the international Mother Nature project. Looby lives and runs courses at Applewood Permaculture Centre in Herefordshire, UK. cultural-emergence.com · @LoobyMacnamara

Louisa Rodrigez (p. 69) is a consultant, facilitator and mountain leader living in the Lake District, UK. When not at work you can find her adventuring, fell running and wild swimming all of which provide inspiration for her writing. Writing, nature and running have been an important part of her healing from Post-Traumatic Stress. Instagram: @louisa.rodriguez

Louise Devlin (p. 88) lives with her three children on the outskirts of Glasgow near fields, streams, and sisterly Beech trees. She works as a psychotherapist and shamanic practitioner, working with people in 1 to 1 capacity and in group settings. immramatherapies.com · Instagram: @immrama_therapies

Lucy Baena (p. 124) is a writer, sea swimmer and mother birthkeeper. She lives in Brighton with her husband and two daughters. Lucy is Autistic and disabled. When she is not in the Sea Lucy is busy looking after her children and spinning words full of Ocean storms, salt and birth blood. Instagram: @lucybaenadoula

Lucy H. Pearce (pp. 1, 76, 161) is the author of twelve life-changing non-fiction books for women, including four #1 Amazon bestsellers and three Nautilus Silver Award Winners – *Burning Woman, Medicine Woman* and *Creatrix: she who makes*. She is a sought-after speaker and teacher on women's creativity and spirituality. She founded Womancraft Publishing in 2014 and the Creative Magic podcast in 2024. A mother of three teens, she lives in Cork, Ireland. lucyhpearce.com · Instagram / Facebook: @lucyhpearce

Lyn Thurman (p. 45) is an author, priestess and a tarot and oracle creator based in magical North Wales. She's followed the spiral path of the Goddess for over two decades. LynThurman.com · Instagram: @lynthurman

Mae Wick (p. 117) loves to learn and wants to return to the forests as an old crone. She wants to be brave, forage for food, and learn herbal medicine. She wants to put love out in the world.

Margaret S. Malloch (p. 37) lives in Scotland. She is currently working on issues around the memorialisation of injustice which has included a lot of thinking about what justice might actually be. Studying campaigns to remember those accused of witchcraft in Scotland. stir.ac.uk/people/255704

Contributors

Martha Trudi Ryan (p. 67) is a visionary artist and multidisciplinary creative from Dublin, Ireland. Inspired to express the truth and beauty of the human experience through her impactful artforms, Martha believes that our deepest painpoints can transform our purpose and that the 'light at the end of the tunnel' is waiting for us inside. martha-ryan.com Instagram: @marthartha

Mary Cardenas (p. 46) Using the ever-evolving soundtrack she curates for her own life as inspiration for the themes she puts on the page, Mary's creative hunger extends to novels, scripts, short stories, and essays. Forever a wanderer… Mary currently resides in Montana and works at her alma mater. marycardenas.com · Instagram: @marycardenaslit

Mary Lunnen (pp. 12, 17, 112) lives near the dramatic coast of North Cornwall, in the far SW of the UK, with her husband and cat. Her passion is helping people find their way home to themselves and rediscover their inner wisdom. She is a writer, artist and lover of the land and ocean. daretoblossom.co.uk · Facebook: @mary.lunnen

Maureen Nadeau (p. 57) is a mother, mixed media intuitive artist and creative guide living in the US. She is the founder of The Soulful Creative where she hosts circles for women who want to connect to their inner wisdom through the creative process. Her work is a celebration of the rhythms, cycles, and seasons of the natural world and all the magic they hold. maureennadeau.com · Instagram: @Maureen_Nadeau_Art

Melissa Rose Spencer (pp. 82, 151) is a Social Worker, Breathwork Coach and Holistic Counsellor who weaves somatic and creative approaches into her practice. All her offerings are underpinned with heart and a solid foundation in trauma awareness. She loves pottery, honeybees, starlings, nettle and rose and lives in Slaithwaite, West Yorkshire, UK. groundedconnection.co.uk · Instagram: @groundedconnection_counselling

Molly Remer MSW, D.Min (pp. 30, 38, 73) is a priestess, mystic, and poet in central Missouri. Molly and her husband Mark co-create Story Goddesses at Brigid's Grove. Molly is the author of ten books, including *Walking with Persephone, Whole and Holy, Womanrunes, the Goddess Devotional*, and *365 Days of Goddess*. She is the creator of the devotional experience #30DaysofGoddess and loves savoring small magic and everyday enchantment. Etsy / Instagram: @brigidsgrove

Nicola Hurst (p. 102) is a jeweller, using her intuition to design and handmake bespoke pieces. Nicola is also priestess, breathwork facilitator, and sacred ceremony and circle holder. Her heart follows the Wheel of the Year; Mother Nature and Grandmother Moon inspire her Becoming as life unfurls daily. nicolahurst.co.uk · Instagram: @_nicolahurst_

Nicola Lilly (p. 115) is a writer and artist based in Ireland. Unfulfilled in accountancy, Nicola felt drawn towards energy healing. Her work involves healing for individuals, hosting circles and teaching Reiki. Currently a SAHM committed to personal healing, her world is filled with creative exploration and learning to honour the Sacred Feminine. Instagram: @nicolalillyartist / @sacredfemininewisdom

Nicole Cohen (p. 40) inspires women to remember their sacred selves, reclaim their goddess power and create change from a place of courage and self love. Using a unique blend of goddess journeys, myths and archetypes, creative facilitation, sacred ritual and self exploration to empower and inspire. She currently lives in England. magicalmuses.com

Nyx Lugrâ (p. 96) is a forty-one-year-old Proto-Celtic songwriter who lives in Wales. In 2010 she was diagnosed as being on the autism spectrum. Her poems reflect on the theme of 'reconnection' from a feminist perspective, and carry hope that a more animistic worldview will enable healing for all beings.

Philippa Aspey (p. 42) is a Brighton based psychotherapist, workshop facilitator and self-taught artist/musician. She believes that every individual has a right to experience meaning, purpose and joy and their lives, and is passionate about co-creating a fulfilling and sustainable future for humanity and our planet. navigatingtheself.co.uk · Facebook: @safespaceworkshops

Pippa Grace (p. 64) is a socially engaged artist, writer and sculptor. A passionate feminist, she specialises in working with women, exploring issues including: the female body, motherhood, maternal lineage, creativity, trauma and sexual violence. Pippa published *Mother in the Mother* with Womancraft in 2019. Pippa lives in Bristol, UK. one-story.co.uk · Instagram: @pippaonestory

Poppy Connor-Slater (pp. 26, 79) lives in York, UK, and loves to create art of all kinds including poetry, painting, drawing, sculpture and textiles. She often finds herself returning again and again to the themes of mythology, folklore, and womanhood which are endlessly fascinating to her. Instagram: @dove.daughter

R.B.L. Robinson (p. 141) is a writer and poet, specialising in nature, creativity, and wellbeing. Through her writing, she inspires people to reconnect with nature and reweave a sense of wellbeing and wonder into their everyday life. She is the author of *Reconnect, Grow, Restore: A Beginner's Guide to Rewilding Your Soul*, *The Enchanted Grove: Woodland Poems to Rewild Yourself*, *Wildcrafted Words: Nature Poems for the Wheel of the Year* and *Thrive: A Slow and Mindful Living Journal for the Wild at Heart – A Life Purpose Workbook, Planner, & Daily Diary Inspired by Nature*.
rblrobinson.wixsite.com · author Instagram: @woodland.wordsmith

Rachel Glueck (p. 22) is a recovering nomad rooting down in Scotland. She's the author of the award-winning, philosophical cookbook, *The Native Mexican Kitchen*. Her greatest loves are walking alone through Scotland's forests and her wise and joyful six-year-old daughter. She currently works as a content manager for a Scottish distillery. rachelglueck.com · Instagram: @reroot_rewild

Rebecca Houston (pp. 54, 60) is a former social worker turned poet who has been scribbling angsty musings in corners with night lights since she was a little girl. Her poetry explores themes of mental health, desire, sexuality, relationships, motherhood, feminism, and social justice. Instagram: @alittlespacetoholdalot

Rhiannon Hasenauer (p. 80) is a witch from Tacoma, Washington. As an avid motorcycle enthusiast and builder, she works to connect the worlds of witchcraft and motorcycling, creating a unique community for both. She owns a business called Motherline Magic where she creates courses, events, and tools for Biker Witches. motherlinemagic.com · Instagram: @thechopperwitch

Rosalie Kohler (pp. 48, 111) is a nature-inspired artist, writer and yoga nidra facilitator who dreams into the stories of the Living Earth singing beneath our feet. Passionate about rest, wild swimming, cyclical wisdom and rewilding the Feminine, she lives with her family in the Black Forest. spiralshores.com · Instagram: @spiralshores

Ruth Everson (p. 108) is a published poet, life coach and international speaker who weaves these threads together to help people live into the most powerful versions of themselves. Poetry is the mirror that reflects who we are. It is a path through inner landscapes. Instagram: @everson.ruth

Sarah Durrant (p. 20) is a poet and learning facilitator living in Norfolk, UK. Her work is an exploration of the many ways we suffer as humans due to our often unconscious mental, emotional, somatic and behavioural patterns, and an expression of her growing understanding of our potential to heal, grow, transform and flourish. sarahdurrant.co.uk · sarah@sarahdurrant.co.uk

Sarah Featherstone (p. 139) is an artist, writer, and trainee Gestalt psychotherapist based in Cardiff. Her work practice encompasses visual art, writing, and educational facilitation and engagement. She is passionate about how creativity can support wellbeing. sarahjfeatherstone.com

Sarah Robinson (p. 150) is an author and yoga teacher based in Bath, UK. She has published many books with Womancraft Publishing including *Yoga for Witches, Yin Magic, Enchanted Journeys, Kitchen Witch, The Kitchen Witch Companion* and *The Witch and the Wildwood*. She loves exploring the power of myth, magic and story. sentiayoga.com · Instagram: @yogaforwitches

Shirley Graham (p. 49) is a feminist academic, teaching at George Washington University's Elliott School of International Affairs. Her writing focuses on gender, militarism, peacekeeping, violence, trauma and silencing. She is the founder of the Student Consortium on women, peace and security. Originally from Dublin, she lives in Washington D.C.
geia.elliott.gwu.edu/geia-director · LinkedIn: @shirley-graham-4707936

Suzanne Dance (p. 145) lives in Edinburgh,Scotland. Suzanne is an eco-feminist, Actor and Community Worker. She is also an Ordained OneSpirit Interfaith Minister. Suzanne has lived her whole life to contribute to her own liberation, and the liberation of women and girls, and for a just, peaceful, rebalanced and restored Earth.
interfaithfoundation.org/minister/suzanne_dance · activeinquiry.co.uk

Vanya Leilani (p. 148) is a depth psychologist, writer, teacher and storyteller. She holds a PhD in Depth Psychology. She has trained with Dr Clarissa Pinkola Estés and served as adjunct professor at Pacifica Graduate Institute. Originally from Brazil, Vanya lives in the Pacific Northwest of the US. Her first book, *The Flesh and the Fruit: Remembering Eve and the Power of Creative Transgression* was recently published by Womancraft Publishing. Her podcast is Belonging to the Wild. Drvanyaleilani.com · Instagram: @drvanyaleilani

Victoria Nangle (p. 23) writes poetry and short stories. She has been an arts journalist for twenty years, working in print, online, local television and radio, specialising in comedy but also covering other arts events and performers in music, art, and the theatre. Instagram: @vickynangle

About Womancraft Publishing

Womancraft Publishing was founded on the revolutionary vision that women and words can change the world. We act as midwife to transformational women's words that have the power to challenge, inspire, heal and speak to the silenced aspects of ourselves.

We share powerful new voices with new visionary ideas, empowering our readers to actively co-create cultures that value and support the female and feminine. This to us is deeply exciting and powerful work.

Womancraft Publishing is a small, independent publisher, founded in 2014 by Amazon-bestselling author, Lucy H. Pearce, and is based in East Cork, Ireland. Our authors are based in the US and Europe, and several of our titles are in multiple languages – nine so far, from Polish to Chinese.

Our books have been endorsed by many of our heroines...and heroes: Oriah Mountain Dreamer, Glennie Kindred, Dr Jean Shinoda Bolen, ALisa Starkweather, Naomi Lowinsky, Steve Biddulph, Dr Michel Odent, Lynne Franks, Phyllis Curott, Thomas Moore, Jeanine Cummins...and treasured as "life-changing" by women around the world.

What sets our books apart is their focus on women's lived experience. We value Feminine ways of knowing – the intuitive, the sensory and sensual, the embodied and personal revelation – as valid and valuable ways of knowing the world and ourselves. Our books centre the personal voice of the author as woman, grounded in her research and intellectual knowing – modelling woman as an authority in her own life, something so often dismissed, belittled or silenced in our culture.

To support this, we offer many free online communities connected to our titles, so that you can continue the journey of discovery in the company of like-minded women, long after you have closed the covers of the book.

As we find ourselves in a time where old stories, old answers and ways of being are losing their authority and relevance, we at Womancraft are actively looking for new ways forward. Our books ask important questions. They are not a wholesale refusal of our current cultural authorities – science, organised religion, academia – but rather saying, "yes and…" What is missing from these perspectives? Who is missing? How partial are these current ways of knowing? What else is needed to ensure we have a more holistic understanding? What lies beneath which has been silenced or ignored? The answer to most of these questions is the female and the Feminine. This is what our books centre.

We aim to share a diverse range of voices, of different ages, backgrounds, sexual orientations and neurotypes, seeking ever greater diversity, whilst acknowledging our limitations as a very small press. Each of our books is chosen personally by Lucy, and is hand-crafted through a creative and collaborative midwifery process.

At the heart of our Womancraft philosophy is fairness and integrity. Creatives and women have always been underpaid: not on our watch! We split royalties 50:50 with our authors. We offer support and mentoring throughout the publishing process as standard. We use almost exclusively female artists on our covers, and as well as paying fairly for these cover images, offer a royalty share and promote the artists both in the books and online. We pay above the living wage to our employees and provide flexible working practices that centre family, menstrual and health needs. We pride ourselves on being fair, open and accountable. Our books have been #1 Amazon bestsellers in many categories, Nautilus and Women's Spirituality Award winners.

Whilst far from perfect, we are proud that in our small way, Womancraft is walking its talk, living the new paradigm in the crumbling heart of the old: through financially empowering creative people, through words that honour the Feminine, through healthy working practices, and through integrating business with our lives, and rooting our economic decisions in what supports and sustains our natural environment. We are learning and improving all the time. I hope that one day soon, what we do is seen as nothing remarkable, just the norm.

We work on a full circle model of giving and receiving: reaching backwards, supporting Treesisters' reforestation projects and the UNHCR girls' education fund, and forwards via Worldreader, providing e-books at no-cost to education projects for girls and women in developing countries – over half a million readers so far. We donate many paperback copies to menstrual education projects, red tents, women's groups and women's libraries around the world including: India, South Africa, Haiti, USA, Canada, UK, Ireland and France... As we grow, we can give more back.

We build alliances with independent, women-run media outlets in order to share our books and help promote and support these important publications. We speak from our place within the circle of women, sharing our vision, and encouraging them to share it onwards, in ever-widening circles.

We are honoured that the Womancraft community is growing internationally year on year, seeding red tents, book groups, women's circles, ceremonies and classes into the fabric of our world.

We are the change we want to see in this world. Thank you for your presence in making this dream a reality.

We invite you to join our Womancraft Facebook Community Group...to connect with other readers and our authors...as well as dedicated Facebook groups for readers of: *Creatrix; Yoga for Witches; Medicine Woman; Burning Woman; The Way of the Seabhean; She of the Sea* and many more.

Do join our mailing list to receive our free digital care package, as well as exclusive pre-order offers and discounts.

womancraftpublishing.com

Also from Womancraft Publishing

Burning Woman
Lucy H. Pearce

The bestselling and much-loved title from Lucy H. Pearce. A breath-taking and controversial woman's journey through history – personal and cultural – on a quest to find and free her own power. *Burning Woman* explores:

- Burning from within: a woman's power – how to build it, engage it and not be destroyed by it.
- Burning from without: the role of shame, and honour in the time-worn ways the dominant culture uses fire to control the Feminine.
- The darkness: overcoming our fear of the dark, and discovering its importance in cultivating power.

This incendiary text was written for women who burn with passion, have been burned with shame, and who at another time, in another place, would have been burned at the stake. **2017 Nautilus Award Winner in the program's 'Women' category of books for and about Women's journey.**

Descent & Rising: Women's Stories & the Embodiment of the Inanna Myth
Carly Mountain

Descent & Rising explores real stories of women's descents into the underworld of the psyche – journeys of dissolution, grief and breakdown precipitated by trauma, fertility issues, loss of loved ones, mental health struggles, FGM, sexual abuse, birthing experiences, illness, war, burnout…

This is territory that Carly Mountain, psychotherapist and women's initiatory guide, knows intimately, and guides us through with exquisite care and insight, using the ancient Sumerian myth of the goddess Inanna as a blueprint. She maps not only the descent but the rising and familiarises us with a process of female psycho-spiritual growth overlooked in patriarchal culture.

Digging for Mother's Bones: a guide to unearthing true feminine nature

Coco Oya Cienna-Rey

Do you hear Her calling? Softly, oh so sweetly, edging you home.

Digging for Mother's Bones is a clarion call, an awakening for women who are ready for a new evolutionary edge of growth. This is a powerful guidebook to bring us home to The Great Mother – the regenerative force of creation, She who is the cosmic womb, the feminine aspect of the divine; so that we may unearth the wisdom of our bodies as living libraries and remember how to be the wisdom-keepers that can resurrect Her bones.

Through visionary words, transmissions of feminine wisdom, practical exercises and hard-lived realities, Coco Oya Cienna-Rey takes us by the hand, and guides us through the darkness and the great joy of reclaiming our connection with Her. Her story is a universal one of trauma, disconnection and navigating the mother wound (as both mother and daughter), on a path to reclaiming sexual sovereignty, reconnecting to ancestors through the motherline and embodying true feminine power.

The Flesh and the Fruit: Remembering Eve and the Power of Creative Transgression

Vanya Leilani PhD

The Flesh and the Fruit is an invitation for us to learn to live more freely in our nature, to believe in our beauty and inherent worth rather than in a poisonous tale of our fallenness and depravity, and to challenge the hierarchical systems of power over that sever us from ourselves, from each other, and from the Earth.

Part mythological exploration, part cultural commentary, and part personal memoir, The Flesh and the Fruit shows us the power of creative transgression as we move toward new ways of being and living. Dr. Leilani empowers us to find our own knowing, permission, and blessing as we walk out of the "shoulds" and into our own nature and wildness.

Yoga for Witches

Sarah Robinson

Find your magic on the mat! *Yoga for Witches* explores a new kind of journey, connecting two powerful spiritual disciplines, with enchanting effects! Witchcraft and yoga share many similarities that are, for the first time, explored in combination, in this groundbreaking new title from Sarah Robinson, certified yoga instructor and experienced witch.

Yoga for Witches shares exercises, poses and the knowledge you need to connect to your own special magic and inner power.

Mother in the Mother: looking back, looking forward – women's reflections on maternal lineage

Pippa Grace

Diverse, rich, celebratory, challenging, sometimes painful and ultimately uplifting together the stories in *Mother in the Mother* illuminate how the strength of maternal love can have the power to heal and overcome adversity.

Whilst much has been written about the complexity of the mother/daughter relationship, *Mother in the Mother* explores new territory by looking at the three-way relationship between grandmother, mother and child. Featuring the voices of over 50 mothers from a diverse range of ages, cultural backgrounds and experiences exploring themes of: love, stress, loss, healing, belonging, infertility, mental and physical health issues, twin pregnancy, adoption, pre-maturity, sexuality, single motherhood, young motherhood, abortion, maternal ambiguity and long-distance relationships with families of birth.

Walking with Persephone : A Journey of Midlife Descent and Renewal

Molly Remer

Molly Remer invites us to take a walk with the goddess Persephone, whose story of descent into the Underworld has much to teach us. This book is a journey of soul-rebuilding, of putting the pieces of oneself back together.

Walking with Persephone weaves together personal insights and reflections with experiences in practical priestessing, family life, and explorations of the natural world. It advocates opening our eyes to the wonder around us, encouraging the reader to both look within themselves for truths about living, but also to the earth, the air, the animals, and plants we share our lives with.

Part memoir, part poetry, part soul guide, Molly's evocative voice is in the great American tradition of sacred nature writing.

Wild & Wise: sacred feminine meditations for women's circles & personal awakening

Amy Wilding

Wild & Wise is not merely a collection of guided meditations, but a potent tool for personal and global transformation. The meditations within beckon you to explore the powerful realm of symbolism and archetypes, inviting you to access your wild and wise inner knowing. These compelling meditations are suitable for reflective reading, or to facilitate healing and empowerment for women who gather in red tents, moon lodges, women's circles and ceremonies.

Use of Womancraft Work

Often women contact us asking if and how they may use our work. We love seeing our work out in the world. We love you sharing our words further. And we ask that you respect our hard work by acknowledging the source of the words.

We are delighted for short quotes from our books – up to 200 words – to be shared as memes or in your own articles or books, provided they are clearly accompanied by the author's name and the book's title.

We are also very happy for the materials in our books to be shared amongst women's communities: to be studied by book groups, discussed in classes, read from in ceremony, quoted on social media… with the following provisos:

- If content from the book is shared in written or spoken form, the book's author and title must be referenced clearly.
- The only person fully qualified to teach the material from any of our titles is the author of the book itself. There are no accredited teachers of this work. Please do not make claims of this sort.
- If you are creating a course devoted to the content of one of our books, its title and author must be clearly acknowledged on all promotional material (posters, websites, social media posts).
- The book's cover may be used in promotional materials or social media posts. The cover art is copyright of the artist and has been licensed exclusively for this book. Any element of the book's cover or font may not be used in branding your own marketing materials when teaching the content of the book, or content very similar to the original book.
- No more than two double page spreads, or four single pages of any book may be photocopied as teaching materials.

We are delighted to offer a 20% discount of over five copies going to one address. You can order these on our webshop, or email us at info@womancraftpublishing.com

Blog plans:

Modron article.

Jan – promoting Modron

Feb – concentrate on Brigid and start to intro Irish stuff – Magic of snowdrops

March – April – promoting Mabon

Pagan Dawn article.

Blodeuwedd article.

* Who is Mabon?
* Houndlords in Celtic myths
* The Maiden's Mabon – Virgin mothers and divine sons
* Do a piece on Gloucester, the Severn Bore, Nodens and Mabon.
* Also start bringing in folk magic and herbs.

May – July – Modron, Mabon & Áine

* Mary (as Modron) as Queen of May
* The Great Boar Hunt in Arthurian myth
* Áine & Midsummer rites
* Deeper explorations of mother & son motif
* A piece on Mary Magdalene

Sep – November – promoting Áine
* Selkie, Fairy Bride & Domestic Violence
* The Dark Maiden
* The Leanan-Sidhe

Book plans:

* Airmid - Celtic Goddess of Herbs & Healing
  - Chapter by chapter on website
    — Dec - May. Publish Autumn 2026

* <u>Irish Folk Magic</u>

  ✓ try
  * Llewellyn
  * Moon Books

  * History (inc. Travellers)
  * Folklore and Fairies
  * Saints and Angels
  * Mary, Mother of God
  * The Old Gods & ~~New Goddesses~~ the New (Ancestors and Spirits)
  * The Round of the Year
  * Daily Blessings

* <u>Deep Green ~~Spirituality~~ Witchcraft; Nature Spirituality as a Way of Life</u>

  ✓ try
  - Llewellyn
  - Moon/Earth
  - Weiser
  - Watkins
  - Bear & Co

  * The green roots of religion
  * Nature spirituality today
  * Deep Green Divine
  * An Enchanted Environment
  * Connecting with the Presence/s around you
  * Circles and spirals of time
  * Tending to the Garden
  * Returning to the Wild

Spinning Her Silver Wheel

* Women of the Mabinogi → based on my article series at Fa.R. Expand to create a long chapter on each. Overcoming trauma & patriarchy etc. Modron & Mabon are the centre.

Arianrhod
Lleu — Healing / trauma

Cauldron
Modron — centre
Mabon → Grail

(also Rhiannon & Pryderi in the Third Branch)

Cerridwen
Taliesin
Creativity / theft.

Rhiannon
Pryderi — Justice / betrayal

Branwen
Gwern
Love / grief

↓ definitely try Llewellyn & Weiser for this.